FAITHFUL ORGANIZING

Devotions for a Christ-Centered Business

FAI✝HFUL
ORGAN✝ZERS

FAITHFUL ORGANIZERS

Faithful Organizers®

FAITHFUL ORGANIZING:
Devotions for a Christ-Centered Business

Cover image ©Audra Steadman

Cover Design & Interior Typesetting by Vanessa Anderson at NightOwlFreelance.com

Printed in the United States

Paperback ISBN-13: 978-1-949193-31-2

TABLE OF CONTENTS

About Faithful Organizers®

The first informal gathering of what would eventually become Faithful Organizers took place during the 1992 NAPO (National Association of Productivity and Organizing Professionals) Conference. At that time, the group was called Christian Professional Organizers. We would meet in hallways, hotel rooms, restaurants, and hospitality suites—anywhere we could!

In 2001, Linda Ely established FaithfulOrganizers.com, a virtual association of Christian professional organizers. At the 2006 NAPO conference, a core team prayed for direction, with the outcome that the members of Christian Professional Organizers and FaithfulOrganizers. com decided to combine visions to become one organization known as Faithful Organizers.

Today, Faithful Organizers is international in scope and remains dedicated to its founding principles. Each Faithful Organizer professes a love of Christ and a commitment to uphold the group's Code of Ethics.

Members of Faithful Organizers consider our organizing businesses to be a part of our ministry. We are a Christ-centered community of professional organizers serving our clients with honesty and courtesy, upholding our Christian values, and honoring each God-given opportunity.

We meet virtually on a monthly basis for a devotion written and led by a member. Each devotion is designed to inspire, encourage, and challenge us in our work with our clients and in our personal lives. We offer a program called Faithful Friends, in which members can meet in small groups for prayer, Bible study, and encouragement. In addition, we offer webinars on a variety of topics of interest to organizers.

The committee that has worked on this book to prepare it for publishing would like to dedicate this book to the founders of Faithful Organizers: Jean Furuya, Barbara Hemphill, Eileen Koff, and Sandy Wright. You can find out more about each of the founders by reading their testimonies in the Founders' Witness Testimonials section of the book. Thank you, founders, for allowing God to use you to create this wonderful group. We are so grateful for each of you!

About this Book

Since 1992, Christian professional organizers from across the country and the world have been gathering virtually or in person to study God's word and to encourage each other in their organizing businesses. True to the nature of an organizer, Faithful Organizers members have kept records of the devotions that were shared over the years. These monthly devotions and the support of a community of believers have been a lifeline for many.

I was fortunate to discover Faithful Organizers a few years after I launched my organizing business. While attending my first NAPO conference (National Association of Productivity and Organizing Professionals), I heard there was a small group of Christians that met early each morning before the first conference sessions began. The next morning, I joined the group for a devotion and prayer. Afterwards, most of us sat together at breakfast and got to know each other, our business successes, and our challenges. I was hooked!

Before becoming part of Faithful Organizers, I had never considered my organizing job to be an essential part of my service to God. Living out this mission has made all the difference in the world! Our monthly devotions are a highlight of my month. Faithful Organizers is such a blessing, and I treasure the friendships I have made within this group.

This book contains a variety of well-received devotions from over the years. Each devotion was written specifically for Christian professional organizers by a Faithful Organizers member. You'll find the author's name in each devotion, and information about each author in the "About the Authors" section. Authors with multiple devotions in the book have most likely volunteered as Education Director at some point. Our authors range from those who are new to the organizing profession to those who worked for many years and are now retired.

If a specific devotion particularly inspires you, I encourage you to reach out to the author. We love connecting!

Better yet, join us! You'll find a welcoming community of like-minded individuals who'd love to get to know you. You can find out more about us, as well as a membership application, on our website: faithfulorganizers. com.

Our prayer is that these devotions will inspire, encourage, and challenge you as you serve your clients and serve God.

With much love,
Angie Hyche, Certified Professional Organizer® (CPO)
Faithful Organizers Education Director, 2020-23

FAITHFUL ORGANIZING

Devotions for a Christ-Centered Business

Wasted Time
Tracy Axcell

"A little sleep, a little slumber, a little folding of the hands to rest—and poverty will come on you like a thief and scarcity like an armed man."
Proverbs 6:10-11 (NIV)

There is a tool I use in my business that opens the eyes of clients to the hours of wasted time in their day. They keep a timer running as they go through their day and note how long it takes to accomplish certain tasks, as well as the time they use for "non-billable" activities. They are all surprised at how much of their workday is wasted.

You and I are no different. However, I'm not talking about our businesses; it's our life of service to the Lord that we can end up wasting. We've been given 24 hours to accomplish all that we can, but too often we waste those precious moments. I like The Message's way of communicating Solomon's wise words: *"A nap here, a nap there, a day off here, a day off there, sit back, take it easy."* In today's world, I suppose Solomon could have said, *"Internet here, Facebook there, TV watching here, sports there."* Ouch. And the end result of wasting time on useless things is, *"You can look forward to a dirt-poor life, poverty your permanent houseguest!"* Proverbs 6:11 (The Message)

God has given us time, and it's valuable beyond measure! Time is to be used for daily work to provide for our needs but also to do His will. Paul tells us that time, if it's not used for His glory, is *"wood, hay, and stubble,"* and

1

will be burned up with no possibility of reward. *"It will be revealed with fire, and the fire will test the quality of each person's work. If what has been built survives, the builder will receive a reward. If it is burned up, the builder will suffer loss but yet will be saved—even though only as one escaping through the flames."* I Cor. 3:13b-15 (NIV)

Today, will you check your day and watch for wasted time? Choose activities that build up His Kingdom with *"gold, silver, and precious stone"* and remove the useless *"wood, hay, and stubble!"* It takes diligence and a willingness to do something different, but God will honor a day used for His kingdom. And ultimately, we will have the joy of laying our crown of rewards at the feet of our Savior, Jesus Christ!

What Are You Trusting In?
Angie Hyche

"Some trust in chariots and some in horses, but we trust in the name of the Lord our God." Psalm 20:27 (NIV)

With much fear and trepidation and faith the size of a mustard seed, I launched my professional organizing business in 2016. Although the first few years were wonderful in many ways, I struggled with bitterness and discontent.

I had poured countless hours into marketing my business. I literally did "all the things" I could think of to promote it, including being a member of my local chamber of commerce, posting on multiple social media platforms, volunteering for nonprofits, writing monthly organizing articles for two local newspapers, attending networking events, giving monthly organizing demonstrations on a local TV talk show, and numerous presentations. In short, I had done just about anything I could think of to build my business, but it hadn't grown.

Yes, I'd had successes—a few great clients and lots of local recognition. But overall, the results were quite disappointing. The return on my investment of time and money was nowhere near what I had anticipated or felt that I deserved. The constant yearning for more left me feeling empty and ignored. Four years of discouragement is a heavy load to carry.

In desperation, I finally decided I HAD to give up control of the results. If I didn't hand this frustration over to God, I was afraid the discouragement would break me. So I started praying more earnestly for God to give me what I needed and to trust Him, no matter how much business I got. I literally cried out to my Heavenly Father.

Along with my decision to trust God, I started putting less time into my business and pouring more time into Bible study, prayer, my family, self-care, and volunteering. I wanted to prioritize what really mattered and to see with eyes to the eternal.

Soon, I started noticing a pattern. When there were inevitable slow times, a circumstance would arise requiring my help. For example, when my stepfather needed major surgery, my business was slow, so I was able to travel with my parents for the surgery. When I was discouraged, I would (uncoincidentally) get an inquiry from a new client that would lift my spirits. This pattern continued so persistently that I knew without a doubt God had intervened each time.

"Some trust in chariots and some in horses, but we trust in the name of the Lord our God." Psalm 20:7 (NIV)

We might not be able to relate to trusting in chariots and horses today, but this verse in Psalm 20 is timeless. Trusting God doesn't come naturally. It's easier to trust in what we see and in things we have control over (or think we have control over). In my organizing business, I had been trusting in my marketing plan, my ability to persuade people with my message, my networking skills, my chamber membership, and so much more. I can't rely on any of those things. God alone is trustworthy.

What are your horses and chariots? What are you trusting in? Be honest about the answers. The simple act of confession—"telling the truth" to God—is powerful. Commit to fully trusting Him. He NEVER disappoints!

I'm so glad we can trust God! If we focus on Him first and foremost, He will give us everything we need. His ideas of what we need might not match ours. But we can trust that God alone understands what's best for us. Our Father really does know best!

God's Plans or a Better GPS
Donna J. Roland

"For I know the plans I have for you," declares the Lord, "plans to prosper you and not to harm you, plans to give you hope and a future." Jeremiah 29:11 (NIV)

I know He has the plans. I just wish I had a better GPS.

Do you ever get frustrated and wonder if being a professional organizer is really what you are supposed to be doing with your life? It can be hard when you walk into a home or office and it is a total wreck and you wonder if you will ever help them get through it! Or you work with a client one week and you go back the next and not much progress has been made.

I have used this verse many times when speaking to people who have been in unfortunate circumstances, and I was trying to reassure them. Then the time comes when I find myself wondering if I am doing what I am really called to do and I have to remember these words that have come out of my own mouth so many times. Sometimes it is a lot easier to say them to others than to understand them for yourself.

Thank goodness I do know deep down He does have plans for me. However, I sometimes wish He would put them on one of His billboards so I could make sure to see it. Or maybe send me an email, leave me a voicemail, or even post it on my Facebook wall!

Unfortunately, it takes more than looking at our GPS and hoping the directions just pop up or deciding you are tired of waiting and just moving forward on your own. I'm afraid I hear that dreadful word "recalculating" more than I care to admit.

As professional organizers, we are also business owners, and I think we can sometimes become discouraged and wonder if we are following the plans He has laid out for us. That is where our faith comes into play. We must study His word and kneel in earnest prayer and listen to what He is telling us. It may be through our daily devotions, a Sunday morning sermon, or through a friend's sweet voice. The Holy Spirit talks to us in many ways, and all we have to do is be willing to patiently listen.

He has called us according to His purpose to help others with our services and expertise in their times of need. We can't take this responsibility for granted and should consider it a privilege to serve by using the gifts He has given us. When the clutter may seem overwhelming to others, it is a welcomed challenge to us.

If He knows every hair on our head, He certainly knows the plans He has for us, and He wants us to have hope and only desires the best for our future. In today's world there are so many people hurting because they feel their future is unknown (or they feel they are buried in the clutter—physically and emotionally) and they have no hope. Fortunately, we know the One that has it all mapped out, and no electronic device is needed.

Psalm 23
Beverly Clower

"The Lord is my Shepherd; I shall not want." (ESV)

The Scottish minister John McNeill (1854-1933) said that he was often surprised at the *converting power* of the 23rd Psalm, as it does seem to be written by and for believers. It is certainly a soothing condolence for anyone who believes in the Lord. We hear it repeated at funerals of innocent children and other beloveds, and on film at the gravesites of Mafia godfathers and society's questionable citizenry. The presence of death can be chilling to a lost soul.

Psalm 23 is much more than a gift of sympathy and comfort; it is an offering of promise, security, wholeness. The first verse alone is an affirmation of life with Jesus. The words burst with ownership, confidence, and blessed assurance that everything is alright, already, right now. In personal and business life, others can sense the "something different" which they don't know is the presence of the Holy Spirit with those in the fold. When their mouths water, they might say one of the following: "Why do you do this?; It must be hard trying to please other people every day; What keeps you so patient?; Where do you get all this energy?; You are an angel." The response can give them a peek inside the gate—a first step in evangelizing. Yet these observations about our persona as we work are, to some degree, an acknowledgement that they see something extra, something different. They want some of it.

My Shepherd

Jesus tells us to trust in him and he will make our path straight. (John 14:1; Prov. 3:5-6). No university, no philosophy or school of thought has ever come close to the promise contained in the context of those Scriptures. Nobody cares about sheep more than their shepherd. Most of us who've ever come upon a herd of sheep or cows blocking the road can recall our helplessness to do anything about it and our annoyance at the delay. When the shepherd comes, he ignores the inconvenience and quietly, gently prods those *in his care* to safety. A professional organizer can think of a client as a person in their care, rather than "I'm in charge here." Our job description is one of service, after all. Isn't that how the Great Commission works?

There are times when our Shepherd has to summon sirens and experts to our rescue, but more often, we can thank Him at the end of the day for hard lessons, trials, small triumphs, being needed, petty aggravation, opportunities to help others, and griefs to unload into His arms. And on top of everything, He forgives our mistakes, our wrong-doings, our misspoken hurtfulness. What a gift to share with those in our care! Take a moment now to praise God from whom all blessings flow.

Many people scoff at the sheep comparison ("I'm not a dumb animal!"), yet sheep share many characteristics of intelligence and awareness with other animals and ourselves. What's important to remember is that Christians in leadership positions have a leader themselves—the Good Shepherd, who sees the good in the sheep and the goats, or he would not have called us to serve.

I Shall Not Want

A worthy mantra on its own. Oh, how we stress over needs regarding our God-given service vocation. "Oh, dear, I have no more appointments after Tuesday." That's a marketing time slot and opportunity that Jesus has already prepared—your chance to give needed attention to children and spouse or to schedule that overdue medical appointment. And when you have overbooked, it is your privilege to own your business responsibilities. With discretion, a couple of those appointments can be changed. Some clients might even be relieved. Admit it, occasionally, when a client reschedules, you're actually glad. That's how God works sometimes. Jesus alone knows our struggle for balance between family, relationships, and work. He wants to manage our time.

The Shepherd is our provider of everything—beautiful dwellings, personal peace, guidance, love, mercy, courage, and safety. He is our all in all. He longs for us to think of Him first and bring to Him our bundle of wants and supposed needs. David understood this when he wrote Psalm 23, long before *"the Word became flesh and made his dwelling among us."* John 1:14 (NIV)

Pray now for a closer relationship with your Shepherd, and thank God for the gift that supplies all our needs.

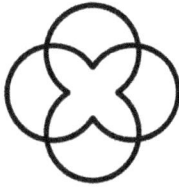

Remembering the Star

Barbara Hemphill

"When they saw the star, they rejoiced exceedingly with great joy."
Matthew 2:9 (ESV)

O ne year in the fall, I had been waking up in physical pain for several nights, but far worse, in deep emotional pain. It had been more than four months since I had a horseback riding accident and broke my collarbone. Although the orthopedic doctor assured me that surgery was unnecessary and I would be back on the horse in November, I couldn't perform the simplest physical tasks without pain. As a result, I had made no progress on several significant projects, which I thought God had called me to do! At night when I woke up, my mind often fell into progressively more profound despair. Would I be physically able to execute the plans on my December calendar, including our annual family Christmas party for 25 people and an important business trip to California that had been planned for many months?

Our church was preparing to host an outdoor movie called "The Star." Our next generation pastor asked volunteers to make "star cookies" to pass out during the event. I didn't have a star cookie cutter, but I grabbed a bag of various cookie cutters in the grocery store at the last minute. (Procrastination? Who, me?!) When I opened the bag, I discovered, "No star!" There was a mitten, a bell, a stocking, a reindeer, a tree (at least that's what I think it was!), and a snowflake, but **no star**! How could it be? Just one more indication of how wayward our culture has become. Despite what revisionist history today would have us believe, our nation was founded on Biblical principles, and the one symbol of the gift that God gave us—his Son—missing!

That night, as I lay awake, fighting the negative thoughts bombarding me, I realized that I, too, had forgotten the star. "But God"—one of my favorite two-word phrases in the Bible—showed up! The sermon the following day was "The Star: A Journey of Hope." The pastor described three steps to help anyone who was struggling during that Advent season:

    1) Acknowledge the darkness.

    2) Embrace the wait.

    3) Commit to the journey.

He recommended three simple Advent prayers:

    1) Each time you recognize some area of darkness:
      "Jesus, shine your light here."

    2) Each time you find yourself annoyed by waiting:
      "Jesus, work on me while I wait."

    3) Each time you hear a Christmas carol:
      "Jesus, help me love you more, as you love me."

After church, a woman with whom I enjoyed working on church projects and whom I had not seen for many years came up to me and asked, "How are you?" Much to my embarrassment, I cried and said, "Not so well." She asked me for more details, and I shared some of them. I acknowledged that part of my despair was my upcoming 75th birthday and feeling overwhelmed at how many things I had started in my life with great enthusiasm, but how few I had finished.

Her response was once again a "But God" experience. She said, "Well, maybe God created you to start things that other people could finish. I'm not very good at starting things." I stood there feeling astounded. You see, one of the projects I had started was offering a new coaching service as a "Vision Accelerator" designed to help people identify and begin executing a vision about which they have been dreaming. One woman had been thinking about writing a book for 17 years, another wanted to go to graduate school for decades to become a counselor, and another had entrepreneurial dreams but felt too afraid to leap.

As I pondered my situation, I was comforted by Romans 8:28 (KJV): *"And we know that all things work together for good for those who love God and are called according to his purpose."* I also recalled what I often tell my clients and the consultants we train: "It will all turn out in the end. If it doesn't, it isn't the end yet." Thank you, God, that it isn't the end for me—or for you! For years I've said that I planned to give a speech on my 100th birthday, but since COVID, I've made a change. My new vision is to live each day "remembering the star," and to encourage those around me to do the same.

Rotten Fruit
Beta Shad

"But the Holy Spirit produces this kind of fruit in our lives: love, joy, peace, patience, kindness, goodness, faithfulness, gentleness, and self-control. There is no law against these things!" Galatians 5:22-23 (NLT)

When food spoils, it becomes stale and unhealthy. What happens when one of the fruits of the spirit becomes spoiled? Can joy become rotten? The answer is yes. Joy is one of the nine fruits of the spirit, and it is the closest fruit related to gratitude. When joy becomes spoiled and rotten, it turns into something called entitlement. This is when someone believes that they deserve all great things, privileges, and special treatment. Entitlement is the opposite of gratitude. When someone lives with an attitude of gratitude, they express appreciation for even the smallest blessings and are completely happy with what they have. They will live to return kindness to others instead of being "me, me, me" focused, constantly wanting more and more from others.

Children these days have it all—endless on-demand shows, movies, and episodes to watch; dolls, cars, and superhero action figures to play with; closets full of swimsuits and clothes for every occasion; social calendars packed with extracurricular activities, birthday parties, and playdates. Organizing all of that is one thing, but is having all of these things neatly arranged in bins and baskets the solution for overwhelmed parents? In addition to all of the physical and digital things kids have today, they are also constantly showered with love, attention, and praise from family and friends. Too much stuff, attention, and over praise can cause a child to feel entitled, which can lead a child to think they deserve to have everything they want simply because they want it when they want it and it better be like right now—or else! This makes it difficult for parents to say "NO!" Hence the pileup of toys and endless entertainment. Then, when all the toys and things accumulate, we lose control of our environment.

In the beginning of my organizing career, I was trying to figure out my ideal client. I didn't know who that was yet, but I did know that I absolutely did not want to organize any toys or playrooms! At the time, I was dealing with an abundance of toys in my own home with my then six-year-old. Although relatively organized, there seemed to be toys everywhere, all crammed into one room and throughout our small apartment. The last thing I wanted in my work life were more playrooms and toys to sort through and arrange. Maybe it was my calling, because now four years later I am thrilled to work with children and have the opportunity to teach them responsible behavior and decision making. By helping moms, dads, and caregivers take control of their household environment, I am also helping them set their children up for success.

"Discipline your children, and they will give you peace; they will bring you the delights you desire." Proverbs 29:17 (NIV)

Things like labeling toy bins for easy clean up, putting healthy snacks at eye level in the pantry, and developing a daily task schedule are ways you can arrange the physical spaces in the home to be kid friendly. This will allow kids an opportunity to successfully do things for themselves, which will, over time, shift the self-centered mindset to gain a sense of independence, responsibility, and hard work. Parents can help their kiddos feel grateful for what they have and avoid the entitlement bug by enabling them to contribute to the family and to their own lives whenever possible.

"Dedicate your children to God and point them in the way that they should go, and the values they've learned from you will be with them for life." Proverbs 22:6 (TPT)

With the best of intentions, moms and dads want to provide their children with a carefree magical childhood. They care so much about their kids' safety, comfort, and self-esteem, but what if our kids' sense of entitlement comes from their belief that we (parents, caregiver, nanny, authority, teachers) are their personal servants? It's not wrong to help our kids out, offer occasional praise, and give them what we might have never had when we were growing up, but the important thing is to set them up for success in life and give them exactly what they need that most benefits their personal relationship with Jesus. He is God's free gift to us and way better than any new toy or video game. With a controlled environment, decluttered and functional for kids, we can help them follow His example of humility and service for years to come.

A High Calling
Eileen Koff

"For the Scripture says to Pharaoh: 'I raised you up for this very purpose, that I might display my power in you and that my name might be proclaimed in all the earth.'" Romans 9:17 (NIV)

This scripture is referring to Pharaoh, but I will take the liberty to say that each of us has been raised for the very purpose of your high calling. In every circumstance you are called into, His name is to be proclaimed on all the earth.

An organized life is a life that flows freely. Our calling as organizers is to introduce or reintroduce that freedom into our clients' lives. Creating an organized environment does more than allow them to move and think unencumbered; it opens them up to a greater understanding of priority and purpose. Understanding "priority" is highly desired by the world. Many magazines have the headline "get organized" somewhere on their cover. Many times, our clients cannot prioritize even the simplest of tasks, and our transference of skills enables them to see what is important or unimportant. Purpose is much harder to identify, but that is ultimately what we do as Faithful Organizers, to mirror and reflect God's glory so that they see the greater purpose for their lives.

This process is like going through a refiner's fire for many. In the silver refining process, heat is applied. The silver and the impurities separate. The pure silver settles to the bottom, and the impurities rise to the top where they can be skimmed off. The refining process brings impurities to the surface (now easily seen, what was once difficult in the dark) so they can be removed.

Our organizing sessions are like this fire. A cluttered and dysfunctional space clogs visual purpose, not only in their space, but also in God's intended purpose for their lives. Clients begin by separating the trash from the treasures, or those things that are no longer needed or of little value. Then they are discarded and removed. Many times, this is an agonizing process, just like the heat of a fire. But in the larger picture, God is refining their space and at the same time refining their hearts so that He can begin to move into their lives. Their purpose, once kept in the dark, is now easily seen.

I can think of no better gift than to allow the Holy Spirit to work in our clients' lives. Giving them the space outwardly and inwardly will allow Him to speak clearly into their lives. These gifts of love that God so lavishly gives to us are translated when our client's purpose is revealed. Faithful Organizers do not come in and make a space nice. We are honored to be sent by God to accomplish not only our purpose, but to help our clients' lives reflect God's purpose for them. Walking on the path of purpose set before us by God brings us immeasurable blessings. I pray that as you give the gift of order to your clients, their purpose is made manifest.

Shine Like Stars
Eileen Koff

"Those who are wise will shine like the brightness of the heavens, and those who lead many to righteousness, like the stars for ever and ever. But you, Daniel, roll up and seal the words of the scroll until the time of the end. Many will go here and there to increase knowledge." Daniel 12:3-4 (NIV)

At the end of days—no, not today, but at the end of all days—we will stand before our Savior and King Jesus and give an account of our time on Earth, be it five seconds or 120 years. I believe each one of us will tell a story of how we were given a great talent and calling to see His order become reality in the lives of those He called us to serve.

In the maddening pursuit of knowledge, and the byproduct of clutter that happens as a result, many are now becoming disillusioned and are asking one simple question: "What is truly important?" Professional organizers have many ways to illuminate the answers to that question. Here is where I see the fulfillment of our calling.

"Those who are wise will shine like the brightness of the heavens and those who lead many to righteousness, like the stars for ever and ever."

In this overly cluttered world, I believe God is not only speaking to those who win souls for Christ in Daniel 12:3, but also to those who are setting a foundation to equip others to bring souls into the Kingdom. When our environments are in order, when distractions are kept to a minimum, when peace prevails in our homes, then we can hear His voice because distractions are no longer winning the shouting game.

The same thing applies when we help a client create an orderly atmosphere where new possibilities and opportunities can open up for them to fulfill their calling. This is achieved by eliminating worldly distractions and empowering them to manage themselves and their environment so that they can hear from God and see their dreams and God-given talents and gifts used to their fullest potential.

One day, at the end of days, all earthly things will pass away. All of our color-coded filing systems, label makers, and organizing storage bins will be extinguished, and a new earth will be created. Will our labor on earth have meaning? All things will pass away, and what is truly lasting and of value *will* last for eternity. We have a unique opportunity to bring God's peace to our clients through our methods and teachings.

When speaking to other professional organizers, I am able to convey that my profession is also a ministry given to me by God. I explain that the goal is not only to create an orderly home, but one that supports and allows my clients to fulfill the calling and purpose that God has given to each individual. I know that God has opened a door to reveal His love and special calling on my life through helping others.

If you have an opportunity, go outside at night and look up. I doubt you'll see the heavens' full display of beauty, but if you can, keep in mind that God created the heavens and the earth, and He has counted each star and given it a name.

"The heavens declare the glory of God; the skies proclaim the work of his hands. Day after day they pour forth speech; night after night they reveal knowledge." Psalm 19:1-2 (NIV)

Christ gives us wisdom to create order and His peace that passes all understanding so that His love can shine through us to each client we serve, and for every situation. We may never know on this side of heaven how many lives we have influenced, but be assured that you will shine in glory, as bright as the sky above.

Sin Clutter
Tracy Axcell

"Jehoiada then made a covenant that he, the people and the king would be the Lord's people." II Chron. 23:16 (NIV)

Clutter builds over time, slowly and consistently, until one day you realize you're living in what feels like a disaster zone! As a professional organizer, I've witnessed this over and over. No client has ever said, "It just happened overnight!" No, they all say the same thing, "It's been building for years!" It's when they finally feel hopeless and despondent that they'll reach out for help.

Sin also builds over time, slowly and consistently, until one day you realize you're living a life that feels like a wreck! It builds up over time and eventually you must face it—you can't help but recognize its destructiveness in your life. At that point, when you can no longer face it, you reach out to the Lord for help in dealing with your sin-cluttered life.

I love how Jehoiada, the priest, dealt with his community of "sin clutterers!" He called every one of them together as a group and recommitted them to the Lord and His work:

"Jehoiada then made a covenant that he, the people and the king would be the Lord's people." II Chron. 23:16 (NIV)

Then he made them deal with the sin clutter in their lives—they had to do the work—they had to go tear down the idols they'd allowed to be built up! *"All the people went to the temple of Baal and tore it down. They smashed the altars and idols and killed Mattan the priest of Baal in front of the altars."* II Chron. 23:17 (NIV)

We all have that sin nature—the old life that wants to fulfill its selfish desires. But we do have the choice to not allow that old nature into our lives! By renewing our minds with God's desires and consistently confessing sin, we keep our lives free of "sin clutter." *"Do not conform to the pattern of this world, but be transformed by the renewing of your mind. Then you will be able to test and approve what God's will is—his good, pleasing and perfect will."* Rom. 12:2 (NIV)

Physical clutter and sin clutter both draw you in with their initial charm—things that no one will see, things that you just can't resist! Both can be ignored or dealt with. Both will negatively impact your life. But only one affects eternity—sin!

It takes hard work to keep sin clutter from building up in our lives! But we can handle it. We can choose to tear down those idols that take position in our life, positions that belong to God! We can choose to destroy whatever pulls our hearts away from our High Priest, Jesus Christ! And then we can recommit ourselves to being the Lord's people!

Deal with sin daily and you'll never have to worry about it becoming clutter in your life!

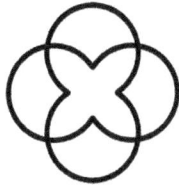

Stewarding and Organizing
Go Hand in Hand
Danielle Wurth

At the beginning of each year, our family takes a fresh look at prioritizing our lives. The Lord entrusts us to steward, honor, and respect what He has given. The same godly principle applies to all the things we buy, store, or even hoard in our homes. This stewardship concept is represented in the Parable of the Talents in Matthew 25:14-28. We are called to practice being a daily gatekeeper of our material possessions by asking, "Do I truly NEED to keep this item with which the Lord has blessed me?" A "yes" answer commits us to respect it rather than throw it in a pile. A "no" answer means to purge accordingly with a giving heart.

From unused serving trays to extra sheet sets, from excessive clothing to children's toys, from office supplies to household tools: they all carry a value and purpose. If an item consistently remains unused and it no longer serves a purpose in your household, then it's best for that item to be passed onto another household who can readily use and appreciate it. When I (or my clients) have challenges making such decisions, I imagine a cross on the item. I honestly ask myself, "Am I truly stewarding this item respectfully?" This approach moves the focus away from my wants and toward what is best for the item. To keep our family accountable to this stewarding spirit, I keep a reusable shopping bag in each person's closet and a household tote in the garage for consignment or donation. The Lord teaches us to share the gospel, not hoard it all for ourselves. The same concept can be applied to our things. Stewarding and organizing concepts go hand in hand and can be passed from one hand to another. In this spirit, the things with which the Lord has blessed us will become a blessing again.

A few thoughts to ponder and pray about:

- What items in your home and/or business do you feel compelled to reevaluate and steward more intentionally?
- How can you encourage clients to view their possessions from a perspective of spiritually stewardship vs. property ownership?
- What are some approaches you can take to separate your (or your clients) "must have" items from "maybe I don't need" items? Have you considered boxing it up and placing it in a separate space as a trial? Sometimes time and a trial provide us the answer.

Be an Encourager
Barb Eimer

"Therefore encourage one another and build one another up, just as you are doing."
I Thessalonians 5:11 (NIV)

I have been in the organizing business for ten years, and if I could tell fellow organizers one thing, it would be this: **Be an Encourager.**

Many times, our clients are depressed and down on themselves. They feel like failures because they can't do something as "simple" as keeping their homes organized and clutter-free. They have bought into the lie that they are worthless, whether Satan put that into their head or someone else did. They can't see past the outward struggle to the heart of the situation.

We know that a huge part of our job as organizers is to listen—not just so we know how to make the space work, but also so we can help our clients deal with bigger issues.

Several years ago, I was helping a lady clear out a large storage unit. Both of her parents had passed away, and one day we found her dad's ashes in a container in the back of a unit. Of course, she burst into tears, calling herself the worst daughter on the planet.

If only you could meet this woman. She is kind and good-hearted and always tries to do the right thing. She had a rough childhood with abusive, alcoholic parents, and then went through a painful divorce that she didn't instigate. I often tell her that she is beautiful and valuable, and that God loves her.

I do wonder, however, if anyone else ever encourages her. She has three teenagers, and we know how appreciative that age group can be! I joke, but she's in a rough spot, and God brought me into her life for way more than to help her get organized.

What she needed most was a friend. Someone to listen without judgment. Someone who would pray for her. It has been two years since I've worked with this woman, but I still text her words of encouragement and pray for her weekly. What have you been called to do?

Are You Hoarding?

Tracy Axcell

"For just as each of us has one body with many members, and these members do not all have the same function, so in Christ we, though many, form one body, and each member belongs to all the others. We have different gifts, according to the grace given to each of us." Romans 12:4-6 (NIV)

Hoarding is a hot topic today! There are many TV productions, magazine articles, and news shows—all depicting the pain and sadness of hoarding. The truly sobering thing about hoarding isn't only the waste—it's the negative effect hoarding has on both the one who hoards and their loved ones.

But, lest we get too self-righteous about hoarders, I have to ask, "Are you hoarding?"

You may not have multiple toasters or keep the stereotypical pile of newspapers, foil, or used grocery bags, but there's still a chance you are hoarding.

You see, we are all unique, and through our uniqueness, we have been given gifts from the Lord that he does NOT want us to hang onto—gifts we are supposed to use and invest in every day. But too often, we're found hoarding instead of sharing those gifts.

In Matthew 25, Jesus is teaching the disciples about His return (and He hadn't even left them yet—no wonder those poor guys were so confused!).

Jesus begins to share the "Parable of the Hoarder." Now, don't run off and Google "Jesus and Hoarders;" you won't find it. But, in vs. 14-30, Jesus talks about three men who were given "talents" and expected to use and invest them wisely.

Two of the men did what they were asked; they used and multiplied what was given to them. But the third man hoarded his talent! This man buried what the Master gave him. And the Master wasn't happy! Why? This servant disobeyed and wasted the Master's possessions. So, what little he had was taken from him, and he was cast out.

In my journey with the Lord, there have been times when I've not "invested" my spiritual gifts as well as I should and chose instead to hoard them. The sad reality is that when we hoard spiritual gifts, they become tools in the enemy's hand! He can tempt us to take our gift of encouragement and turn it into jealousy of others, or our gift of exhortation he can use as a tool to condemn others. He'll take any chance he is given to distort and destroy the beautiful gifts God has given! So when we hoard, we're doing exactly what is seen on every TV show about hoarders—we're destroying the value and usability of that gift!

I praise God for His patience and grace during my times of hoarding His gifts! He forgave my sin of disobedience and misusing His gifts, and He provided more opportunities to use and multiply His gifts.

Just like the three servants in the parable, you and I are entrusted with precious spiritual gifts. We are expected to invest and multiply those gifts through the power of God's spirit:

"For just as each of us has one body with many members, and these members do not all have the same function, so in Christ we, though many, form one body, and each member belongs to all the others. We have different gifts, according to the grace given to each of us." Romans 12:4-6 (NIV)

If you are convicted that you've been "hoarding" your spiritual gifts, confess that sin! Jesus' blood covers all our sin, but the Father is waiting for His children to admit their sin and their willingness to move back to living as an obedient and faithful servant. You have time today to begin investing in the work of the Lord. Ask Him to show you how and where to use your gifts—the investment will pay off!

Hoarding or investing—what will you do today?

Loving Our Home
Kimberly Bignon

"The thief comes only to steal and kill and destroy. I came that they may have life and have it abundantly." John 10:10 (ESV)

A few weeks ago, I arrived at the home of a darling new client so eager to begin, excited for change, and yet overwhelmed by the thought of the process—getting from the mess to the victory. The internal battle was raging, but the glimmer of hope for something new was evident in her eyes.

We had a brief consultation walk-through and then dove in that day. After a few hours of tackling her young boys' room, we stopped for a lunch break, and I said a prayer. I prayed over our meal, for our hands' work, and that our work would create a safe, welcoming haven for her family to live in daily. I prayed for all who would enter as guests to feel the love and welcome of the Holy Spirit in her newly organized home, free from the burden of years of clutter. And as I said amen, I looked up and noticed that she was weeping.

She said to me, through a stream of tears, "I have been given so many wonderful gifts in my life. I have a part-time job that affords our lifestyle and so many wonderful things, but I'm not enjoying them at all. In fact, I'm so burdened by the things in my home that I don't love my home either." Week by week, we tackled the mountain of clutter and unorganized living and began letting go of the excess, creating spaces that made sense—

spaces that said "welcome." And we talked about the importance of loving our home well.

If Jesus were to knock on the door of your home, would you, like Martha, have the confidence to open your home to Him? Would He be pleased with how you care for the good gifts he has given you? Doesn't He own everything anyway? If so, how are you caring for HIS things? Loving our home well is tough for so many people. Life is busy. Kids are messy. Husbands are messy. The temptation to NOT buy more is a struggle. How to manage the flow of stuff is a battle. When our hurried lifestyles collide with our immediate needs, and everything we need is buried under clutter, we buy more because we don't know what we already have. And so, the maddening cycle begins—we end up with a cluttered home, a life we aren't loving, and a home that isn't being loved well.

The thief enters our homes to steal, kill, and destroy. But Jesus came that we would have life and life to the fullest! (John 10:10) When we invite Him fully into our lives and homes, we can live well, say "welcome" with confidence, love others well, and breathe deep sighs of relief when He comes knocking at our door. He sends his helpers disguised as professional organizers to help set the captives free. He loves them in the middle of their mess, but He loves them too much to leave them there.

You will be happy to know that the darling young mom took back her home, LOVES her home, and spends more time with people and less time dealing with piles. She has claimed victory over the enemy territory of clutter. Glory! She opened her heart to change and her home to Jesus and found some new courage along the way.

As organizers, we have an opportunity that many pastors and counselors do not have. When the door opens to our smiling faces— disciples disguised as "home changers"—little do our clients know that they are also inviting Jesus into their homes. I pray that they will know us by our love and by the gifting of the Holy Spirit we have been given to teach them how to love their homes well.

All glory to The One who loved us first.

Gratitude Changes Your Attitude
Michelle Kuiken

It's no coincidence when the same theme and message keep popping up all over the place. God uses all sorts of people, events, and conversations to show you what He wants you to be learning. Recently, God has been showing me the importance of giving thanks and teaching me how integral gratitude is for His master plan.

I am in awe of how gratitude is not only powerful, but extremely necessary. Having a mindset of gratitude allows us to experience the goodness God has in store for us.

When I was little, I was taught to always say please and thank you. "Thank you" became an involuntary response to things, a response that I didn't even think much about other than it being courteous to others and being a part of being a Christian. I'd flippantly shoot up thanks to God: "Thank you for my food, thank you for a comfortable house, thank you for a good parking spot…" I think we all would agree that giving thanks to God is important, but would people agree that it's life changing?

The Bible says:

"…in every situation, by prayer and petition, with thanksgiving, present your requests to God. And the peace of God, which transcends all understanding, will guard your hearts and your minds in Christ Jesus." Phil 4:6-7 (NIV)

"Devote yourselves to prayer, being watchful and thankful." Col 4:2 (NIV)

"Let the peace of Christ rule in your hearts, since as members of one body you were called to peace, and be thankful." Col 3:15 (NIV)

"Let us come before him with thanksgiving." Psalm 95:2 (NIV)

"Give thanks in all circumstances; for this is God's will for you in Christ Jesus." 1 Thess. 5:18 (NIV)

"Always giving thanks to God the Father for everything, in the name of our Lord Jesus Christ." Eph. 5:20 (NIV)

Well, I've been learning that gratitude is life changing. The more I offer gratitude, the more I change—my heart, my relationship with God, and my business. And that feels invaluable.

God uses gratitude and the means of giving thanks as a way to transform us. The more we offer gratitude, the more He changes our hearts, and He changes our perspectives.

The main thing that has blown me off my feet is how offering true thanksgiving gives us peace—a God-centered peace about life (Phil 4:6-7). When we can turn our prayers of both suffering and joy into thanksgiving, we are turning our eyes to God and giving Him the credit. And when we do that, He takes it from us and is able to mold our lives.

In my business, when someone cancels with short notice, I am learning to say, "Thank you, Lord." If there is a week when the phone doesn't seem to be ringing and I have expenses to pay, I muster the faith to say, "Thank you, Lord." And in those seemingly negative times, God is able to use me. If my response was frustration, doubt, panic, fear, worry, and all those emotions I naturally feel, I'm closing myself off to God's perfect opportunities to use me. And as much as I don't want to say, "Thank you for no work and flaky clients," I definitely don't want to miss out on the incredible blessings God has in store.

In addition to the discouraging times, it's important to also offer gratitude in the height of business. We need to remember not to take the credit for our success, but to turn to Christ and say, "Thank you, Lord." Those out of the blue speaking opportunities, big budget clients, and exciting breakthroughs during sessions affirm all the hard work put into our businesses and His grace. "Thank you, Lord." The more we offer gratitude, the more our faith grows and the more peace we experience.

Imagine if we could show our clients that by offering gratitude for the items they reluctantly part with and put into the donate bin, that God says He will give His children the peace and blessings they need. "Thank you, Lord."

It can take many circumstances for us to finally soak in what God is teaching us, and I am finally thanking God for showing me the life-changing plan of having an attitude of gratitude. And not just an attitude, but a transformed way of life.

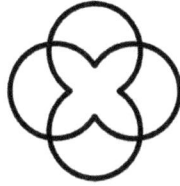

No Place for Pride
Angie Hyche

"You must have the same attitude that Christ Jesus had. Though he was God, he did not think of equality with God as something to cling to. Instead, he gave up his divine privileges; he took the humble position of a slave and was born as a human being."
Philippians 2:3-11 (NLT)

It's time for true confessions. I have had all the following thoughts during organizing sessions:

- "Another day. Another client. Another house full of stuff. How do people live like this?"
- "How does she cook in that kitchen? The counters are completely covered!"
- "Can't he see that if he had regular habits with dishes, laundry and daily pickup, the house would look better? We've talked about that over and over."
- "How do they expect their kids to learn to take care of their stuff if they aren't modeling that?"
- "Did she really believe that buying all those clothes and shoes would make her happy?"

Just typing these is eye-opening. What a terrible attitude!

Pride: The Worst of the Worst

Although I struggle with many different sins, pride is the one I have to constantly fight. The meaning of the word "pride" I'm talking about in this devotion is arrogance, superiority, thinking of oneself too highly. Pride of this kind is not Christ-like.

I find myself looking down on clients for not grasping organizing principles, not being willing to let go of clutter, or not being diligent in their habits. In other areas of my life, I've looked down on people for not taking care of themselves, not valuing a good education, not speaking proper English, or not being assertive (among other things). Cue internal eye roll.

Can you relate? The principles that come so naturally to me as an organizer are completely foreign to my clients. But those same clients who struggle with organization probably have more knowledge and skills in other areas. In addition, I need to remind myself that God is the source of my abilities, not me.

I imagine my tech-savvy husband must feel the same way when he's trying to explain to me (again) how to update my website. He's already explained it plenty of times. In fact, he finally decided to record a video I could consult, so I didn't have to keep asking him. What seems so common sense to him sounds like a foreign language to me.

Of all the sins to which mankind is prone, pride is the one God hates most. The Bible uses all the following words to describe how God feels about pride: oppose, hate, loathe, against, rebuke, tear down, abase, scatter, destroy, cut off, punish, defile, and despise. This strong language connotes strong emotion.

Some would venture to say that pride is the source of all sin. When we put ourselves above others, we are going completely against the Bible. God detests pride so much that He actively *opposes* a prideful person.

"And all of you, dress yourselves in humility as you relate to one another, for 'God

opposes the proud but gives grace to the humble.'" I Peter 5:5 (NLT)

"Because of the privilege and authority God has given me, I give each of you this warning: Don't think you are better than you really are. Be honest in your evaluation of yourselves, measuring yourselves by the faith God has given us." Romans 12:3 (NIV)

The Example of Jesus

If anyone had a right to be prideful, it was Jesus. After all, Jesus was (and is) the Son of God, the very embodiment of God in human flesh. Philippians 2 paints a beautiful picture of Jesus' humility.

"You must have the same attitude that Christ Jesus had. Though he was God, he did not think of equality with God as something to cling to. Instead, he gave up his divine privileges; he took the humble position of a slave and was born as a human being." Philippians 2:3-11 (NLT)

We have more knowledge and experience in organizing than our clients. But we aren't superior to them. If we consider ourselves better and convey a haughty attitude, our clients may sense it. Not only would that damage our efforts to help them, it would damage our ability to show them the love of Christ.

Changing Our Attitude

How can we change our attitude? I don't have all the answers, but I'd like to offer a few suggestions.

1. **Remember to pray.** I'm so thankful that Faithful Organizers taught me the example of praying before client sessions. It's been a game-changer for me! I pray for insight to see solutions for their organizing challenges. I pray for humility, compassion, and understanding so that I can love them like Jesus would.
2. **Remember your own weaknesses.** I purposefully share embarrassing stories with my clients. It's a great equalizer, and it helps my clients see that I am sometimes challenged with disorder too.

3. **Remember the source of your skills.** Any knowledge, ability, and passion we have comes straight from God, not from ourselves. He deserves the glory, not us.
4. **Remember the example of Jesus.** He was the only one who could have rightly claimed superiority. But He didn't. He humbled Himself to put our needs first, to the point of spilling His own blood.

With a humble heart, the power of God's Spirit, and the example of Jesus, we have all we need to adjust our attitude and to show our clients God's love.

This is the Way; Walk in It
Kimberly Bignon

"Whether you turn to the right or to the left, your ears will hear a voice behind you, saying, 'This is the way; walk in it.'" Isaiah 30:21 (NIV)

A few weeks ago, I took my seven-pound Yorkshire terrier, Miles, on a long walk around the lake. Almost every single morning, afternoon, and evening when we take off for our usual stroll, Miles immediately stops and leans in the direction of his choice, digging his paws into the pavement until I go the way he wants to go. Stubborn little bugger.

It is such a perfect visual of how my relationship with the Lord is some days. He is nudging me in one direction, while I keep leaning and pulling in another. You, too? As Miles and I headed towards Lake Ivanhoe this particular day, I insisted on keeping our walk to the land side along the sidewalk. But Miles, all seven pounds of him, kept pulling me towards the lake—it has a lot more dog smells from his neighborhood friends. But I kept yanking him back to the safety of the sidewalk—until finally, I gave in.

No sooner had we crossed the street and taken about eight steps than a HUGE BRANCH (I mean—HUGE!!) came crashing to the ground, directly where we had just been standing. If I had not given in to this stubborn little pooch, we would have both been crushed. I nearly jumped out of my skin, laughed out loud (I think I was in shock), and immediately praised the Lord for His protection. When we arrived home later that afternoon, I gave Miles a treat and crowned him My Hero!

How many times have I found myself in danger's way because I did not yield to the voice of The One who has my best interest at heart? I chose the scripture in the title above to memorize this week as a reminder to my stubborn heart to LISTEN more intently to the voice and gentle nudging of the Lord telling me which way to go. More often than not, it's my pride and self-centered heart that needs some humbling to get me walking in the direction and will of the Lord. Can you relate to the stubbornness I sometimes struggle with? Do you often find yourself in compromising situations, relationships, financial struggles, or dead-end roads?

Buy this house, don't buy that one.

Stay in this relationship, get out of that one.

Stop spending money, save, save, save.

Let go of clutter, be content.

Take this job, don't take that one.

Stop "doing" so much and just "be."

And on and on.

Can I get an Amen?

Perhaps we all need a gentle reminder to LISTEN more intently to the Voice of the Lord behind us, saying, "This is the way" and then move with it!

A client of mine's mother has been in an Alzheimer's facility for a few months now, so I've been helping him clean out her estate. The family is ready to purge, share, donate things, and sell her home. However, the process of going from digging out to selling is taking months. To say hoarding was a problem is an understatement. With all the blessings she had and the love she felt, this sweet woman still had a real stronghold for things—many with tags still on them, shopping, and collecting. We have found numerous notes—too many to count—she wrote to the Lord as prayers or to herself in a journal screaming for help to stop the madness of all the stuff she was buried under. Her husband, who had passed away, was not aware of her struggle and her family enabled the situation, so she kept ignoring the gentle nudges from the Lord to make a change. For years, she could not even enjoy what she had because she didn't know what she had. She was crying out, but she wasn't listening to His Voice and taking the steps necessary to move in the direction of freedom.

Whatever your situation may be today, I am confident of one thing (as I've learned the hard way countless times and the right way other times), the more we know The One we follow, the easier it is to hear His Voice behind us saying, "This is the way; walk in it."

This devotion is a gentle reminder to all of us to spend the FIRST moments of our day listening to, learning from, yielding to, and moving with The One who knows the way we should take!

And guess what? When you yield, you may avoid a huge branch falling on your head.

Thank you, Jesus, for your grace and gentle shoves in the right direction—listening, yielding, and moving with His Spirit.

Trusted with Much
Eileen Koff

"Whoever can be trusted with very little can also be trusted with much, and whoever is dishonest with very little will also be dishonest with much. So if you have not been trustworthy in handling worldly wealth, who will trust you with true riches? And if you have not been trustworthy with someone else's property, who will give you property of your own?" Luke 16:10-12 (NIV)

In sessions with my clients, as well as while presenting at speaking engagements, I am always asked questions like these: Is clutter really a *faith* issue? Does it really matter if I let the endless to-do lists go undone? It's hard to believe that God really cares if I hang up my coat!

I can assure you that, yes, God is concerned! Even when it comes to the tiniest of details. He needs to see whether you can handle the small things before He entrusts you with greater responsibility.

It's the same story time and again—clients tell me they want to have it all, but many hesitate to take the responsibility of caring for it. So many times, I've seen my clients' homes piled high with stuff, but the family is oblivious to the negative effects the clutter has on communication, cooperation, and more.

In every meeting I have with a client, I strive to act as God's hands and feet, His love and influence, into each situation. I teach my clients that when we are responsible for the way we take care of our items, those around us begin to follow suit. I was recently working with a woman whose son repeatedly neglected to straighten his own room. When he saw how his mother and I were working together to organize the rest of the home, his personal habits changed as well. He had simply been waiting to see the "right thing" done to inspire him to incorporate the same changes. Never ever underestimate the smallest of actions.

"Every action in our lives touches on some chord that will vibrate in eternity." — Edwin Hubbell Chapin

We must always strive to do what is honorable and just—not only with our actions, but also with the items that God has provided. Only then will we be able to receive and manage the true riches He wants to give us.

I pray that, personally as well as professionally, God will equip you to handle each and every circumstance and item to His glory.

Heart Check
Lisa Dodson

"The heart is deceitful above all things and beyond cure. Who can understand it?"
Jeremiah 17:9 (NIV)

What does God say about our heart? Spending time in God's Word will reveal quite a bit about the heart, and it's not all about love and sweet things.

I was having a conversation with a fellow Christian lady, and I told her that I was studying about the heart. I mentioned a key verse about the heart, which says, "the heart is deceitful." I asked her how she felt about that, and her response was, "Well, I don't know about that." She couldn't relate to her heart being deceitful. Honestly, I had to spend some time studying this idea as well.

In Jeremiah 17:10, God states, *"I the Lord search the heart and examine the mind."* God knows all things about every person. Our hearts are deceitful in that we all sin and fall short of the glory of God (Romans 3:23). God points out that our hearts are deceitful so that we will take the time to examine them ourselves. He encourages us to look at our own hearts, not to compare them with others' hearts.

When I brought up to my friend about a deceitful heart, I believe she was thinking, "Well, I haven't done this or that." That's where our pride gets in the way. Because we don't think we are that bad, we don't spend time purifying our hearts so we can look more like Jesus. *"Blessed are the pure in heart, for they shall see God."* Matthew 5:8. Can others see God in you?

Take a look at your heart and pray to the Lord to reveal areas in which you need to grow and improve. This can be challenging and painful. Is He calling you to love more deeply? Forgive an offense? Cast away fear? Love an enemy? So often, the heart issues revolve around love. In 1 Peter 1:22, the Word says, *"Having purified your souls by your obedience to the truth for a sincere brotherly love, love one another from a pure heart."*

Join me in praying from Psalm 51:10: *"Create in me a clean heart, O God, and renew a right spirit within me."* Get stirred up about the deceitfulness of your heart so that you can make some healthy and helpful changes in your life. The Christian life is always evolving, and we strive to be more Christlike.

The Epidemic of Hurry

Angie Hyche

"Still others, like seed sown among thorns, hear the word; but the worries of this life, the deceitfulness of wealth and the desires for other things come in and choke the word, making it unfruitful." Mark 4:18-19 (NIV)

"Be still, and know that I am God." Psalm 46:10 (NIV)

In July 2022, I had a LOT of downtime. It wasn't by choice. My husband, Eric, and I figured it was inevitable, just a matter of time before we finally got COVID-19 too. There we were—stuck at home, just like many others during the pandemic. Although we'd been exposed numerous times, we'd always managed to escape infection before. But not this time.

The timing was pretty rotten. But honestly, is there ever a good time to be sick? We were one week away from the opening night of a community theatre production of "The Sound of Music." It was the first show in five years for me (a very long time), and I was ecstatic to be acting with Eric and around 40 other cast members. We'd rehearsed for eight weeks, three to five nights a week, for several hours each time. That's a lot of hours spent rehearsing! And now we would have to miss the first two of three weekends of performances. Such a disappointment!

On one of those slow days of isolation, I decided to take a walk. I really enjoy walking and praying, so that's what I decided to do that day.

In fact, sometimes I walk and pray only because I'm less likely to mentally rehearse my dance steps for the show or ruminate over my lengthy to-do list while attempting to pray. On this particular day as I walked, I was praying (again) about some big decisions I was in the process of making. It was an oppressively hot day, so I stopped to rest at a small park.

This park is a favorite destination in our downtown neighborhood. My father and stepmother lived in the neighborhood nearby at some point during my childhood, and my sister and I played here frequently. I have distinct memories of attempting to shoot a basketball into the regulation size goal, which seemed enormous at the time. To this day, if I visit the park and there's a basketball lying around, I'll pick it up and shoot for a few minutes just to relive those moments.

I wasn't in a hurry that day, so I reclined on the top of a picnic table to enjoy the breeze and to look up through the oak tree branches with the cardinals and blue jays perched on them. I wondered how big that oak tree had been when I visited the park as a child. How interesting to think that this tree had witnessed my attempts to shoot baskets in that goal so many years ago! Was the basketball goal the same? What about the swing set and the jungle gym—had they changed? I know I certainly had!

This quiet time to think and pray was nothing short of blissful. It was exactly what my soul needed, especially during that season in which I was contemplating big decisions. Taking this time to think and pray was only possible because I wasn't in a hurry that day. Five days of isolation had drastically changed my schedule. And though some of the consequences were extremely negative (like missing performances of the play), for the most part, the change was welcome and much needed.

I recently read (and reread) *The Ruthless Elimination of Hurry: How to Stay Emotionally Healthy and Spiritually Alive in the Chaos of the Modern World* by John Mark Comer. This book is an eye-opener. It had been recommended to me several times before I finally gave in and read it. I can honestly say it's one of the most thought-provoking books I've ever read. I was so challenged by the biblical message of this book that I could no longer procrastinate making some monumental changes in my life. It had been a long time coming.

Hurry has become so much a part of our lives that we've come to accept it. In some ways, we've come to view busyness as some kind of badge of honor, a symbol of our importance. We rush about our days frantically, flitting from one activity to another, anxiously trying to connect all the dots and fit everything in. Our minds race in harmony with this frenetic pace. But do we realize the price we're paying?

As Christians, we strive to follow the model of Jesus. While he certainly had plenty of activity during His time on earth, He was never in a hurry! He was never too busy to meet a need. He regularly and purposely carved out time for quiet reflection and prayer. He knew He needed it. How much more so do we!

I challenge you to carefully consider the way you spend your days. Is busyness wreaking havoc on your soul? Are you too hurried to hear the voice of God and to see the needs around you?

I am going to make silence, solitude, simplicity, and slowing a priority. How about you?

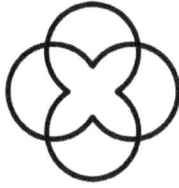

Jimmy Choo Shoes
Eileen Koff

"Then Jesus spoke to the crowds and to His disciples, saying: 'The scribes and the Pharisees have seated themselves in the chair of Moses; therefore, all that they tell you, do and observe, but do not do according to their deeds; for they say things and do not do them. They tie up heavy burdens and lay them on men's shoulders, but they themselves are unwilling to move them with so much as a finger.

But they do all their deeds to be noticed by men; for they broaden their phylacteries and lengthen the tassels of their garments. They love the place of honor at banquets and the chief seats in the synagogues, and respectful greetings in the marketplaces, and being called Rabbi by men." Matthew 23:1-7 (NASB)

A recent client couldn't wait for me to witness her closet. Her wardrobe was the main focus of our organizing session. You could tell she was delighted that this was where she would be spending our time. Upon entering her closet, I couldn't help but notice many designer shoes (some never worn) and designer labels on her dresses and accessories. She seemed almost intoxicated by the fact that the closet reflected an aura of status few could rival.

The professional organizing industry is by nature a witness to what our clients and society value. Our western world hungers to be significant and is willing to do anything to obtain attention. Getting noticed and adored is the hallmark of all advertisements.

Jesus was very clear in his admonishment to the Pharisees in Matthew 23. Their garments reflected their spiritual superiority, and they sought to increase that superiority by the design and placement of the phylacteries and tassels. It was of utmost importance that they project a superior "Rabbi" attitude, ensuring that they would gain respect and obtain all the very best places of honor. Their aim was to be noticed and revered.

Jimmy Choo shoes say much the same—at least they spoke to my client that way. Her hunger for significance is an inherent drive that desires recognition and relational significance. Attempts like hers to find that significance through material possessions are commonly seen within our industry. We not only see them played out in material goods, but in careers, vacation destinations, and friendships. As an organizer, I have witnessed the twisted intent of a world searching for significance without the Lord. At times I have felt a heavy burden for my clients, but I know that as our relationship deepens, their trust in the organizing process will also take on new directions.

The most powerful tool that I bring to every organizing session is a mirror. I become the mirror, reflecting back their actions and thought processes. By restating their words and holding up objects for examination, they begin to see their thoughts clearly. I am continually amazed that God uses this process to change beliefs and habits that have been ingrained for years.

The Jordan River vs. The Dead Sea

Seana Turner

"He said to me, 'This water flows toward the eastern region and goes down into the Arabah, where it enters the Dead Sea. When it empties into the sea, the salty water there becomes fresh. Swarms of living creatures will live wherever the river flows. There will be large numbers of fish, because this water flows there and makes the salt water fresh; so where the river flows everything will live. Fishermen will stand along the shore; from En Gedi to En Eglaim there will be places for spreading nets. The fish will be of many kinds—like the fish of the Mediterranean Sea.'"
Ezekiel 47:8-10 (NIV)

A number of years ago, I had the privilege of traveling to Israel. It was a wonderful trip, though I feel like I only scratched the surface. Everywhere we went I learned something new. My trip was during the month of February, part of the "rainy season," and one day we stopped near the mouth of the Jordan River. I learned that in Hebrew "Jor" means "from," and that the land near the northernmost part of Israel was originally assigned to the tribe of Dan. Hence, the Jordan is the river that flows from the region of Dan. When we were there, the mountain snow was melting and blending in with the rainfall. The river was lush, almost a glacial blue, flowing rapidly down into the Sea of Galilee.

Eventually, the water passes through the Sea of Galilee and further down until it reaches the Dead Sea (a.k.a. the "Salt Sea"). As you may know, the Dead Sea sits far below sea level and has no outlet. As a result, the water just puddles up there and ultimately evaporates into the arid atmosphere of the surrounding desert. The concentration of minerals and salts is intense, such that no living thing dwells inside. From a distance it is pretty, but when you are nearby, it has an eerie feeling of stagnation.

As I stood looking over the misty Dead Sea, I found myself pondering the contrast between the two bodies of water I had seen. The Jordan River is like the Christian life, characterized by endless renewal as the Holy Spirit repeatedly churns away that which weighs us down. We are forgiven and made pure as snow, just like the glacial waters flowing from Mt. Hermon. In contrast, life without God can be dry. The Holy Spirit is absent, sin piles up and eventually life is snuffed out.

In the book of Ezekiel, the prophet is given a vision in which a new river flows from the new temple in the new Jerusalem. This river will flow down to the Dead Sea and restore it to the glory for which it was designed. Trees will again grow upon its banks, and fish will once again dwell inside. The vision is one of promise, giving us hope for the future.

As organizers, we often enter spaces that may seem a bit like the Dead Sea. Suffocating numbers of possessions and overwhelming commitments have entered the lives of our clients. We may see rooms that no longer sustain the activities they were built to accommodate. We may find items that are "dead" and should be discarded. We may encounter souls that have become discouraged and hopeless.

While we cannot offer salvation from sin, we can, like Ezekiel, be a source of hope:
- We can flow in like the Jordan River and help to dislodge and clear out some of the accumulated matter.
- We can bring energy and enthusiasm to those who are stuck.
- We can provide techniques and systems to ensure circulation of belongings.

We can also pray. Some clients may know God, but may simply be struggling to shake the voice of the tempter when it comes to time, space, and stuff. Others may have turned away from God and are wondering if they could be welcomed back. Still, others may never have heard the gospel and are unaware of their need for forgiveness.

As Christian organizers, we have the privilege of flowing where the Spirit moves us. We also have the responsibility to serve Him wherever we are taken. May we drink deeply from the fountain of Jesus Christ, and by doing so, refresh a weary world.

"Let anyone who is thirsty come to me and let the one who believes in me drink. As the scripture has said, 'Out of the believer's heart shall flow rivers of living water.'"
John 7:37-38 (NRSV)

Three Words to Make Your Season:
Simple + Christ = Peace

A Christmas Devotion
Ann Cueva

"Glory to God in the highest heaven,
and on earth peace to those on whom his favor rests."
Luke 2:14 (NIV)

There is a single Christmas decoration on my fireplace mantle this year. It is a 9" x 16" plaque that reads, "Simplify Christmas… Celebrate Christ." Those who see it have the same response—"Oh, I love that; it is beautiful and peaceful." That is what I felt when I first saw it. How quickly it brought the focus to Christ. At that moment, I decided to make it the theme for our Christmas.

It is so easy to get caught up in the Christmas chaos and rush, but as Christians, we need to refocus our thoughts, time, energy, and values as we enter the most wonderful time of the year. Beware if we find ourselves saying, "I am so glad Christmas is over and I can rest," or "I'm exhausted, tired, and broke; I hate Christmas!" And a comment I heard this past July, "Oh no, five months until Christmas; I'm not over last Christmas yet." What a great example we can be for our clients and a great witness for Christ as we show the love, joy, and peace which can be enjoyed by all when our focus is on the right thing.

As an organizer, I often use the word "simple" in planning and performing. Too often many associate Christmas with words like stressful, hectic, tired, broke, depressed, and, for some, dread! This frustrated frenzy results in a man-made Christmas replacing the true meaning and the original, sacred purpose and intent—celebrating our Savior's birth!

Wonder what our Heavenly Father thinks when He watches us run ourselves "ragged" for one day of the year? When He watches you, what does He see? I hope you choose to simplify Christmas. May you enjoy and find the peace that only The Prince of Peace can bring at Christmas and throughout the year.

New Wine and Old Wineskins
Eileen Koff

"Neither do people pour new wine into old wineskins. If they do, the skins will burst; the wine will run out and the wineskins will be ruined. No, they pour new wine into new wineskins, and both are preserved."
Matthew 9:17 (NASB)

Jesus told John the Baptist's disciples that people don't put new wine into old wineskins because the skins will burst, and the wine will be wasted. *"Put new wine into fresh wineskins, and both are preserved."* Matt. 9:17 (NAS). This biblical principle is one that we, as professional organizers, can pass on to our clients. During many of my sessions with clients, I sense that they are stuck, overwhelmed, and unable to move forward. Their clutter has a way of keeping them unable to focus and trapped in a quality of life they no longer wish to continue.

However, it has been my experience that many clients would rather pour their new wine (new organizing methods) into their old systems. They constantly resist the thought of changing their methods and their systems. A simple example is swapping out the placement of kitchen dishes with another cabinet because the space in the old cabinet does not fit the size of the dishes. But, they have been married to their placement for so long, they wouldn't dream of a rearrangement! They want the new wine—a well-organized kitchen—but they sabotage those dreams because they resist the physical change (old wineskins). This is a very simplified example. As organizers, what are we to do?

I'm willing to guess that 90 percent of your clients need a total mental makeover. Our daunting challenge as professional organizers begins with a mental renovation project, demolishing old thought processes before new ones can emerge. The task is not impossible, but it will require us to help our clients take these steps:

1. Break free from the fear of change. Change is inevitable, but there is so much resistance that getting our clients to move forward requires patience and trust. We need to trust God that He will supply you with the insight and words that will penetrate so that they see change as a positive life force. Go slowly. Getting them to adapt to many changes at once will lead to disappointment and frustration. It takes a long time for wine to mature!

2. Be willing to defy tradition. People who are married to the past cannot embrace the future. "That's the way I've always done it," will not work to declutter their life. Choosing what is comfortable for your client will not always work, and here is where the experiment of adopting new procedures comes into play. I will ask my clients to play the "game" for two weeks. Getting them to stretch their comfort zone along with a new mental awareness can produce inspiration and greater changes that were ever expected. I see this not only from the client, but from their families as well.

3. Ask the Spirit to reveal His new strategies. I see through a glass darkly, and coming into any situation, I bring my own lenses. I need God's perspective to shed His light into the true needs of the situation. Pouring my own wine into their new wineskin can also burst the pouch. Seek first His directions through prayer, and trust that the Holy Spirit will reveal to you new concepts, ideas, and strategies that you may never have considered. I'm always amazed how God never lets me down when I ask!

I believe the Lord wants to unleash a gushing river of new wine into those we are called to serve. What is old must be renewed by the Spirit, what is outdated must be remodeled, and what is ineffective must be replaced. God wants to do a new thing. Time to toast with new wine!

A Spacious Place
Kimberly Bignon

"He is wooing you from the jaws of distress to a spacious place free from restriction, to the comfort of your table laden with choice food." Job 36:16 (NIV)

We live in a world full of clutter. We fill our homes with stuff; we fill the hours of our days with activity, noise, and stress. More always seems to be better, and enough is never enough. Waves of distractions quickly snuff out our good intentions of simplifying. Distractions that wage war within us, distractions that the world presents as important, cool, and necessary for survival. Before we know it, we are stuffed to the max, worn to the bone, and often left wondering if anything we do is seriously impacting this world. It truly is a problem that quickly becomes a vicious cycle.

Simplify. Buy more stuff. Simplify. Shop. Let it go. Do more things. On and on goes the cycle. I see it every single day in my job. I see it in my own life. For the past few weeks, I have been on a word search through the Scriptures. Over and over again, the Lord has led me to particular verses that say, "He brought me out into a **spacious place**…"

Fascinated by this phrase, particularly because He keeps speaking it to my heart repeatedly, I did a little research to understand it better. And this is what I discovered—the Hebrew word for "spacious place" is "merchab," which means a broad or roomy place, an expansive place, or a wide place.

Psalm 18:19 states, *"He brought me out into a spacious place; He rescued me because he was delighted in me."* (NIV)

Doing a little further investigation, I found these parallel translations of the same phrase:

"He led me to a place of safety . . ." —New Living Translation
"He brought me out into a broad place . . ." —English Standard Version
"He brought me forth also into a large place . . ." —King James Version
"He set me free in the open. . . ." —New American Bible

This spacious place is a provision from the Lord. It's a stopping place for our hearts, our minds, and our lives to get off the fast track of cluttered living and just rest. It's a place to breathe. It's a place of freedom. He brings us to this place because He delights in us! He truly has our best interest at heart. When we bring our "stuff" out into a WIDE-OPEN place, we can inventory what truly is important versus what seems urgent and necessary in our own eyes. We can breathe deeper, and most importantly, we can see and hear the One calling us to a life of peace in the midst of a busy world.

I don't know about you, but I am thankful for the spacious places the Lord provides me. A place to get off the treadmill of life to breathe, a place to say "no" to more activity with confidence (remembering that "no" is a complete sentence), and a place to walk around barefoot in the grass with Jesus. Today, let's embrace that **large place** of safety and relief, free from the restrictions and burdens of this world. Your clutter does not define you. But how quickly it does take over our lives when we don't take time to stop off in the "spacious place" to be refreshed and renewed in the Spirit.

I'm camping out in these verses for the next few weeks until the Lord and I walk in step with one another in the grass of His priorities for me. Won't you join me in the spacious place? The grass truly is greener over here.

Breathing deep sighs of relief for us all.

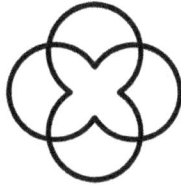

Turn Fear into Gratitude and Peace
Michelle Kuiken

"Then Jesus said to his disciples: Therefore I tell you, do not worry about your life, what you will eat; or about your body, what you will wear. For life is more than food, and the body more than clothes. Consider the ravens: They do not sow or reap, they have no storeroom or barn; yet God feeds them. And how much more valuable you are than birds! Who of you by worrying can add a single hour to your life? Since you cannot do this very little thing, why do you worry about the rest?...For the pagan world runs after all such things, and your Father knows that you need them. But seek his kingdom, and these things will be given to you as well...For where your treasure is, there your heart will be also."
Luke 12: 22-26, 30-32, 34 (NIV)

I was always a worrier when I was growing up. Something in me felt fearful and unsure. My dad would always sing to me at night a song with these lyrics—"Why worry when you can pray, trust Jesus and he'll lead the way. Don't be a doubting Thomas, trust fully on His promise..." This is a song I can still find myself repeating in my head today. Such a simple song and concept, yet hard to fully put into action.

I knew that worrying was not a healthy habit because it seemed to have a strong power over me, a power that seemed uncontrollable. It wasn't until I was older that I started to realize that worry was from Satan, and it was rooted in fear. God tells us not to fear because He will take care of all our needs (v. 32). He knows the desires of our hearts beyond even what we can begin to verbalize to Him (Luke 12:30, 1 Chron. 28:9). How amazing to have a God who knows (and cares) what we need and want!

When I work with clients, I can see that they often operate out of worry and fear. They don't know what to do with their items or spaces, and fear can be what is holding them back.

When we are fearful, we have the auto response of freeze, flight, fight, or fold. Most often, when our clients are posed with a hard challenge, they either freeze and don't make a choice. Or they flee, and still don't make a choice. It appears "easier" to the client to avoid the issue, but fear is driving their actions and thoughts and preventing them from moving forward. After all, fear can stand for False Evidence Appearing Real.

As organizers, we know that clients call us to help them make those hard choices and move them forward to what is real. Many times, it's not until they can uncover what is getting in the way that they can move forward and make hard choices. We are there to be their guide and to help them uncover the fear that is standing in their way. Common fears clients may face include fear they will need the item again, fear they will offend, fear they will forget the memories, fear they won't have enough for tomorrow.

Luke 12 says that worrying cannot add days to our life (v. 25). It can't help us resolve any situation. In fact, worry and fear actually allow Satan to take hold of our minds. Verse 32 tells us not to be afraid! It's a command to hold Satan back.

The song I sang as a child is right when it says that the weapon to getting rid of fear is prayer. Ephesians 6 (the armor of God) also says that in order to have peace, we must pray—and not just pray, but offer thanksgiving! Giving gratitude to God helps our hearts transform from worry to peace and trust.

Verse 34 says that what we treasure is where our heart will be. As productivity specialists and organizers, we can help our clients discover what they treasure as they pull back the layers of fear. We have the opportunity to help them determine what they treasure so they can get rid of the fear, move forward, and find peace. Having a mindset of gratitude is a wonderful place to start!

As we help clients, we can also help our own situations by giving thanks to God in all circumstances through prayer. He will provide, He will protect, and He will take the worry away. So why worry when we can pray and receive peace in the love of Christ?!

Challenge: What is one small way you can help your clients express gratitude in their households? If the situation doesn't allow you to approach it in a spiritual manner, how can you still help them rid the fear and express gratitude? Either way, we can start fighting Satan's lies.

It's About Time. Or Is It?
Allison Mitchell

"Teach us to number our days, that we may gain a heart of wisdom."
Psalm 90:12 (NIV)

I realized in organizing my life, unless I take the TIME to write something down, I more than likely won't do it. This is why I do an evaluation for my clients. They can see their goals. Many clients call us because it would take too much TIME to begin to work with the clutter in their homes alone. Each day I write a few things that I would like to accomplish besides what's on my schedule. I might be speaking to the choir here, but as I check those things off my list, I feel very successful. Can you relate?

Since I like lists and want to be successful in reaching my goals, I occasionally take the time to write them down. Here are my goals in order as I wrote them:

1) Walk 30 minutes every day.
2) Spend time with the Lord every day.
3) Finish work before the kids come home.
4) Lighten up! And get the kids to help!
5) Eat within 30 minutes of waking every day.
6) Be more trusting of the Lord.
7) Seek ways to actively parent.
8) Be more thankful for what I have.

As a part of initiating Goal #2, Spending TIME with the Lord every day, I started reading a book called *Jacob's Dozen: A Prophetic Look at the Tribes of Israel* by William Varner. The book starts off with Jacob being exiled for 20 years because he was unwilling to wait for God's TIMING in his life. Hum, I thought, a 20-year consequence! EEEKKK! Many of our clients' clutter is a 20-year consequence. As organizers, we are there to help them reduce the amount of TIME they are spending looking for lost items or reduce the amount of time it takes to maintain their basic systems.

"Teach us to number our days, that we may gain a heart of wisdom." Psalm 90:12 (NIV)

I need wisdom to number my days, to make things count! I need to take the TIME to eat within 30 minutes of rising. I need to take the TIME to spend 30 minutes walking. I need to make TIME to spend TIME with the Lord. I need to take the TIME to be more thankful for what I have. I need to take more TIME to seek ways to actively parent. I need to slow down in TIME to lighten up. And what about Goal #3, Finishing work before the kids come home? TIME management. It's all a matter of TIME—or is it?

As I have taken the TIME to spend TIME with the Lord (wishing this is what I put for Goal #1), these are the things that start to happen—HE starts reminding me to eat within 30 minutes and walk 30 minutes a day. It doesn't seem like a spiritual task, but it's important in my life, and He knows this. So, if I turn my TIME and attention to HIM first, then it seems like he rearranges the TIME in my day. My days ARE numbered— why waste them in a 20-year consequence? Why not be obedient each day as much as humanly possible? If I give Him my TIME, not a moment will be out of order!

"Walk in obedience to all that the Lord your God has commanded you, so that you may live and prosper and prolong your days in the land that you will possess." Deuteronomy 5:33 (NIV)

My way of applying that verse—Walk in obedience so that you will live, prosper, and have many days in blessings. The land that the Israelites were to possess was a land filled with blessings that would make their lives better and reduce the TIMES of struggle for food or peace.

I don't know what you would write down for your goals right now, but I have rearranged mine. I need to take the TIME to be attentive to Him first thing in the morning.

1) Focus on the Lord (not work, not people, not my day, not my eating)

2) Obey what I hear from focusing on the Lord.

3) The rest....

In my recent study on TIME, I have discovered that the Jewish calendar of 12 months is based on the moon. Then we have 12 hours of daylight and 12 hours of nighttime. I ask you—Who set the moon and the stars in the sky? So, Who holds the hands of TIME? How are you going to spend your TIME this year? How much TIME needs to go into organizing versus your families? Where do you need to be devoted to Him wholly? He wants us to obediently seek Him in the Bible and in prayer.

TIME is irrelevant in His economy; however, OBEDIENCE is essential.

He has no beginning or ending. His consequences can last 20 years, yet it took a long weekend to be sacrificed on the cross and rise from the dead to become our Savior.

Will you let Him be in charge of your TIME?

Friendly Competition
Angie Hyche

"Do nothing from selfish ambition or conceit, but in humility count others more significant than yourselves. Let each of you look not only to his own interests, but also to the interests of others." Philippians 2:3-4 (ESV)

I'm an extremely competitive person. From early middle school through the end of my undergraduate college years, I competed on at least one sports team each year, and sometimes two or three. I've always competed not only in sports, but in just about anything you can possibly compete in. It borders on ridiculous sometimes.

Even though it's been many years since I've participated in team sports, that aggressive spirit is part of my nature. It's both a blessing and a curse—it pushes me to do my best, but it also causes me to have an adversarial attitude towards competitors.

I remember the last time I noticed a new professional organizer in my area. "Oh, great. There's another one," I thought. When I started my business, Shipshape Solutions, in 2016, there was only one part-time organizer in the area. The last time I checked, I think there were eight or nine.

Although most of the other organizers didn't seem to be ambitiously pursuing clients through social media, networking, etc., this new one was different. Her posts looked professional. Although she wasn't a member of NAPO (National Association of Productivity and Organizing

Professionals), she had gotten some training from another group. It looked like she was getting consistent business, and I was struggling. Cue jealousy. And resentment. "God, I've been working SO hard for over five years, and she's getting more clients than me. It's not fair!"

I sat in that uncomfortable space for a while. Too long. I knew my attitude wasn't Christlike. That competitive spirit had reared its ugly head again, and I needed to deal with it.

Thankfully, I was able to pour out my heart to my Faithful Friends group, who encouraged me to contact this new organizer. My first few efforts to reach out were unsuccessful; both email and phone messages went unreturned. I assumed all kinds of untrue things while I awaited a reply.

When she finally got back to me, she was so excited that I had reached out and said she had been thinking of doing the same. She had been following my business for a while and wanted to meet me. We had a wonderful time getting together for breakfast and sharing our stories. She's a Christian as well. We even talked about being peers, not competitors. I've already had an opportunity to pass along a potential client to her that wasn't a match for me. I have no doubt that we will continue to be in touch with each other and will help each other with our businesses.

These verses from Philippians are challenging for someone who is competitive like me:

"Do nothing from selfish ambition or conceit, but in humility count others more significant than yourselves. Let each of you look not only to his own interests, but also to the interests of others." Philippians 2:3-4 (ESV)

Jesus was the perfect example of living out these verses in Philippians 2. He did nothing out of selfish ambition, and He was always looking out for the interests of others. Modeling Jesus is ALWAYS the right choice, even when it doesn't come naturally and it's hard to do. God will reward our obedience.

I'm so grateful that the Spirit led me to contact the new organizer, and that my Faithful Friends group encouraged me to keep trying. As Christian business owners, our rules and values are different from the world's. Praise

God for that! Ultimately, we are all on the same team, God's team. And if she ends up scoring more points than me (I mean, getting more clients than me), I'm even ok with that too.

Tyranny of the Urgent
Eileen Koff

"If you belonged to the world, it would love you as its own. As it is, you do not belong to the world, but I have chosen you out of the world."
John 15:19 (NIV)

Peace…ahh peace. Sitting on a beach, watching the waves crash in hypnotic rhythm on the shore. Listening to a whippoorwill call to its mate in early spring. Finally, time to finish that compelling book that takes you back in time. It's time to unwind, time to drift…

Okay maybe for about 20 minutes, and then it's time to pick up the kids from school, give them a snack, take them to their after-school activities, come home, fix dinner, pick up the kids again, serve dinner, take care of the dog, set the table, eat, decide who finished their homework, who gets to play downstairs for an hour, discuss the bills with your husband, figure out what's important tomorrow and… then (if you're lucky), get to bed before 11 p.m. Just a day in the life of today's woman! It's the tyranny of the urgent, right?

"Just because you can doesn't mean you should" is one of my favorite quotes because it covers a multitude of issues. *Just because* you've been saving this, doesn't mean you should, *just because* you can pile on more activities in the day, doesn't mean you should. What I'm really saying is, "*Just because you can*, doesn't mean God intends for you to do it."

Ouch!

We all agree that our calling to become professional organizers comes from deep inside. I might even be so bold as to say that God placed the desire there, but it's our response to that desire that makes us who we are and is what drives us throughout the day. It seems like most people I know struggle with the same lifestyle I do—too much on their plates and not enough time to do it all. Sadly, we have become a nation of workaholics. That's why vacations are so necessary. It helps just to get out of our day-to-day routines and into different surroundings so we can get recharged.

Remember the story of Lot and Abraham? In Genesis 13, Lot decides to leave his Uncle Abe in search of greener pastures. Due to arguments, Lot and Abe separate. *"So Abram said to Lot, 'Let's not have any quarreling between you and me, or between your herders and mine, for we are close relatives.'"* (vs. 8) *"Lot looked around and saw that the whole plain of the Jordan toward Zoar was well-watered, like the garden of the LORD, like the land of Egypt."* (vs. 10) But what Lot didn't see was that Sodom and Gomorrah were smack dab in the middle of those greener pastures or that how he positioned his tent gave rise to inward desires. In deciding to separate from Abraham, Lot and his family went to live close to the people in Sodom. *"Lot lived among the cities of the plain and pitched his tents near Sodom."* (v. 12) *"Now the people of Sodom were wicked and were sinning greatly against the LORD."* (v. 13) Eventually, Sodom and Gomorrah, where Lot had settled, was plundered, whereupon Lot was taken into captivity with all his goods. Later in the story, Lot and a few of his family members were able to escape God's wrath on Sodom and Gomorrah.

Let's examine what led Lot to desire to live there in the first place. Some would say that it's human nature to desire greener pastures, and it's always easier to fit in than to stand out. Our lesson—we have been called to be *in* the world, not *of* it. *"If you belonged to the world, it would love you as its own. As it is, you do not belong to the world, but I have chosen you out of the world."* (John 15:19 NIV) In other words, if we eye those greener pastures, we will become like the world around us. (The world's urgencies become our urgencies.)

Today's society is so into microwaving that we have forgotten that God is into marinating. He wants to get inside of us, not just get us cooking. By expecting life to be instant (digital clocks, quickie dinners, sound bites), then we move and think at breakneck speed, forgetting to stop.

A dear friend has a wonderful way of stopping. When she's driving and comes to a stop sign, she actually *stops* (really—I know—it's hard to believe). She counts to three, takes a deep breath, and thanks God. She continues to ask for His protection over her wherever she goes. She's then able to concentrate on the here and now. She has also learned the art of prioritizing. (I know why she is a great friend of mine!)

As organizers, we can get so caught up in the world that our priorities can soon take a back seat. It's God who gives us our daily tasks, and just because we can do "x," doesn't mean He calls us to do it. *How do we know the difference?* It starts with listening.

As we spend time getting quiet, listening to our hearts, and listening to or reading His Word, we will know what He wants us to do. I just love it when I get a thought that I have absolutely no idea where it came from— that I need to call a certain someone I haven't seen in 20 years or the need to pray for my neighbor. I chuckle, knowing that it wasn't my idea. I *know* I didn't have them on my to-do list, but it was on God's to-do list for me.

My number one priority is to listen to the still small voice.

What if today's action really counts for your tomorrows? *Just because you can* doesn't mean you should. Throw the urgent out the door and settle down with a great cup of your favorite four-minute brewed tea, some freshly made muffins, and *listen* to the stories your family has to tell—and don't forget to listen for that still small voice!

Professional Christian
Tracy Axcell

"When the people heard this, they were cut to the heart and said to Peter and the other apostles, 'Brothers, what shall we do?'"
Acts 2:37 (NIV)

I've come to realize as a professional organizer that I cannot make people be organized. I can share great ideas, I can even prove those ideas within the confines of their home or office, but I can't make them into an organized person—they have to do it themselves! It requires a complete change from who they were to who they want to become. That change can only be brought about by their willingness to be a different person!

It may be a weak comparison, but I believe the same is true as a Christian. No, I don't call myself a "professional Christian," but the scenario is the same. I cannot make someone be a Christian any more than I can make someone be organized. I can present the truth to them and show them how it can affect their life, but ultimately, they have to make the decision to be a Christian. And like my organizing clients, to become a Christian requires a complete change from who they are to who they want to become. That change can only be brought about by their willingness to be a different person!

In Acts 2, Peter shows us how to best present the truth of Jesus to others, or for our example today, how to be a "professional Christian."

What makes Peter such a great "professional Christian?"

1. He is a true worshiper of Jesus

"When he had led them out to the vicinity of Bethany, he lifted up his hands and blessed them. While he was blessing them, he left them and was taken up into heaven. Then they worshipped him and returned to Jerusalem with great joy. And they stayed continually at the temple, praising God." Luke 24:50-53(NIV)

Peter, along with the other disciples, worshiped the Lord Jesus Christ! It was a part of their life that no one and nothing could stop—they were worshippers of Christ Jesus, the risen Lord!

2. He shared Jesus' story

"Fellow Israelites, listen to this: Jesus of Nazareth was a man accredited by God to you by miracles, wonders and signs, which God did among you through him, as you yourselves know. This man was handed over to you by God's deliberate plan and foreknowledge; and you, with the help of wicked men, put him to death by nailing him to the cross. But God raised him from the dead, freeing him from the agony of death, because it was impossible for death to keep its hold on him." Acts 2:22-24 (NIV)

Peter knew the life of Jesus! He knew the truth, the scriptures, and the story of Jesus Christ. And his focus was on Jesus, not himself. He shared Christ's deity, His authority, His life, death, and resurrection. He shared Jesus' story!

That's it. He was a worshiper of the risen Christ, and he shared the story of Christ Jesus.

But look what happened as a result of being a worshiper who shared Jesus with others:

"When the people heard this, they were cut to the heart and said to Peter and the other apostles, 'Brothers, what shall we do?'" Acts 2:37 (NIV)

"What shall we do?" In other words, those who heard Peter were asking how they too could change and stop being who they were and become who Peter was—a Christ-follower, a believer, a Christian. And he told them what they needed to hear—Repent of your sins, be baptized because Jesus forgave your sins and you will receive the gift that Jesus promised, His Holy Spirit!

Peter didn't make them change. He didn't force them to change. He simply lived life as a worshiper of Christ and told Christ's story.

I may claim to be a professional organizer, but in no way would I claim to be a professional Christian! But I sure would like to be better at it! How about you? As Christians, we all need to be great worshipers of Christ and skilled at sharing His story. In doing so, others will be drawn to Him in such a way that they ask, "What can I do to change? What can I do to become a Christ-follower too?"

Worship the Lord and share His story with whoever will listen. And when someone asks, "What shall I do?" you'll have the added blessing of seeing a life changed because they chose to change—to repent and turn to Jesus!

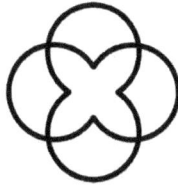

Networking Like Jesus
Angie Hyche

"For the Son of Man came not to be served, but to serve others, and to give His life as a ransom for many." Matthew 20:28 (NIV)

As business owners, most of us are all too familiar with networking. Whether or not you've participated in a formal networking group, you've probably attended your fair share of networking meetings. If you're an introvert, you may dread them. Or you may see them as a necessary evil, something to, hopefully, drum up some business. That was my attitude—until I met Barbara.

This particular networking group met at an assisted living facility. Attendees made small talk and drank coffee before the meeting began. Then each of us gave our 60-second introduction about ourselves and our business. No one timed these intros, so some people took advantage of the opportunity to turn a 60-second intro into a five-minute sales pitch. The meeting droned on. Internally I was rolling my eyes and thinking, "What a waste of time. Why do I keep coming to these?"

During casual conversation after the meeting, I complained (again) about my lack of business and clients who were "ghosting" me. You know how it is—you start working with a client, make some good progress, and then you never hear from them again. Barbara seemed interested in my problem and offered to sit down with me afterwards to brainstorm solutions.

I was puzzled why Barbara, a long-time beauty consultant, wanted to help me. I figured she'd listen for a few minutes and then turn the conversation towards my skin care needs. She didn't. She listened intently to my client issues, asked clarifying questions, told me she knew how frustrating it must be, and then offered sage advice. I was blown away by her selflessness. I asked her why she would choose to give me her time so freely. Her answer changed my attitude about networking.

Like me, Barbara had also been frustrated by networking experiences. Time after time, she gained little return on her investment. But unlike most people, she didn't just stop attending; she changed her focus. When she decided to go for the express purpose of giving and to focus on what she could offer to the other attendees, it changed the whole experience. And—spoiler alert—she started receiving a return on her investment after all.

The real reason this encounter was so meaningful was that Barbara was acting like Jesus. Jesus was never part of a formal networking group. But He was definitely a networker. And he always went to give, not to get.

When Jesus entered a room of people, He wasn't thinking of Himself at all. He didn't hand out business cards or give a rehearsed 60-second elevator speech. Nor was He scanning the audience to find a good candidate for His latest deals. Jesus looked at the people and loved them. By focusing outwardly, He was able to see and meet the needs of the people. I don't think Jesus ever left a crowd of people saying, "Well, I didn't really get anything out of that. I don't think I'll go back."

I want to be more like Jesus at networking meetings, going with the express purpose of seeing the needs and helping others. Even if those interactions don't ever lead to clients, I know I'll be blessed. Yes, I want to grow my business. But more importantly, I want to reflect Jesus to the people around me. I want to be more like Jesus all the time.

The God who Heals
Michelle Kuiken

As my mother was nearing the end of her days on earth, my sisters and I wanted to do something special to honor her in a memorable way. On what ended up being her final Mother's Day on earth, we gathered around our mom and each shared from our hearts one of the names of God from the Old Testament. We chose Jehovah Jireh, the God who Provides; Jehovah Roi, the God who Sees; and Jehovah Rapha, the God who Heals.

Being the youngest, I was stuck with what I thought was the hardest name to swallow in this given situation—Rapha, The God Who Heals. How could I begin to share in an encouraging way about a healing God when it was evident my mother wasn't going to be healed from her cancer?

Well, as God always works in mysterious ways, He helped me see the beauty and lesson in the trying situation.

While studying about the names of God to understand the "God who Heals," God brought me to the passage in Exodus 15 when this name is used. The Israelites who were wandering in the desert desperately needed water, but the water they found tasted bitter. Moses cried out to God, and God told him to throw a piece of wood in the water to make it clean—"sweet" to drink.

"He said, 'If you listen carefully to the Lord your God and do what is right in his eyes, if you pay attention to his commands and keep all his decrees, I will not bring on you any of the diseases I brought on the Egyptians, for I am the Lord, who heals you.'" Exodus 15:26 (NIV)

The word "heals" isn't used in a way that we think in human terms. He heals in a way that is transforming beyond our earthly understanding. God turned what seemed to be bitter into something that would truly satisfy the Israelites' needs. He performed a miracle to meet their earthly needs for water, and He showed them how he wanted to eternally heal their hearts— from bitterness to sweetness.

Through studying this scripture and commentaries, I was encouraged to learn about Jehovah Rapha. The God who Heals created all; He gives and takes away; but it's all in HIS healing. I learned, and later shared with my mom and sisters, about this passage, and we found much peace in knowing that God was in control of her healing. God wouldn't heal her on the earth as I could understand healing, but He was going to give her ultimate healing in the presence of Christ—eternal healing. And this type of healing was going to be well beyond any healing I could have hoped for my mother. And thankfully, His mercies continue to heal my heart as well.

You may be wondering how this ties into our organizing and productivity work? The people we get to work with are people who need to experience the power of our healing God. We all need healing in some way. From bitter to sweet.

Most people who hire us decide to reach out for professional help because of some sort of life transition that has made them aware of their excessive belongings or productivity shortcomings. Usually when people have life transitions, that means hardship or change, and therefore some type of healing is required in the process (whether they realize that at first or not). I've worked with women who are newly divorced, widowed, and empty nesters. They all needed some sort of healing, and my role was to support them in that process with their physical things, while (hopefully) showing God's ability to heal their hearts and situations.

We are privileged to come alongside people and show them that healing is possible. There may be habits to break and years of piles to sort through, but being healed is an option. It looks different for everyone, and some healing may take a lifetime, but God promises to meet the needs of His followers as He sees fit.

From bitter to sweet.

Healing doesn't always manifest as we think it should—like with my mother's health—but it is a process that is done in His will and way. He will help us through the earthly battles, so we are prepared for His Kingdom. And we are privileged to help others along the way.

God wants to use us, like He used Moses, to turn bitter into sweet. How are you helping others turn "bitter into sweet" in their homes, offices, or schedules? How are you representing that sweetness in your business?

May you experience the love of Jehovah Rapha in this season of life.

Giving Thanks

Eileen Koff

"It is good to praise the LORD and make music to your name,
O Most High, to proclaim your love in the morning
and your faithfulness at night,
to the music of the ten-stringed lyre
and the melody of the harp.
For you make me glad by your deeds, O LORD;
I sing for joy at the works of your hands."
Psalm 92:1-4 (NIV)

Giving thanks is at the heart of scripture. The Old Testament is filled with verses referencing the call to give thanks:

"Give thanks to the LORD, call on his name; make known among the nations what he has done." 1 Chronicles 16:8 (GOD'S WORD® Translation)

The New Testament strengthens the Old Testament terminology:

"...always giving thanks to God the Father for everything, in the name of our Lord Jesus Christ." Ephesians 5:20 (NIV)

Giving thanks describes life in the Holy Spirit, a song of praise that is ever bubbling over in the heart. More than a positive outlook, more than a rote prayer, this true thanksgiving is a supernatural, Holy Spirit activity continually giving praise in our hearts to the Father. Our western mindset teaches that thanks is what we exclaim when something has been done for us, such as a gift or favor. Our response is to say thank you. In biblical culture, when it speaks of thanks, the giving of thanks and praise is always addressed to the person of God himself. It gives honor and is an expression of who God is! AWESOME, WONDER, and WOW!!!

Because God is so glorious and fantastic, thanksgiving is an attitude of the heart, a delight like the little child clapping and jumping with abandonment to the necessary response of who God is. Scripture says that this attitude, this applause to God, is expressed.

"O clap your hands, all peoples; shout to God with the voice of joy." Psalm 47:1 (NASB)

Thanksgiving is intentional and deliberate. We are revealing the glory of God. We are declaring it to each other and to the world of darkness by speaking it into the atmosphere. Simply put, thanksgiving is a leap into the arms of God.

I'm sure you are asking yourself right about now "What on earth does this have to do with organizing?" Let me explain.

"For although they knew God, they neither glorified him as God nor gave thanks to him. Instead, their thoughts turned to worthless things, and their senseless hearts were darkened." Romans 1:21 (NIV)

This chapter speaks of the degeneration of mankind when Adam and Eve begin to believe the lie. This chapter in Romans says that although they knew God, they neither glorified him nor gave thanks to him. When Adam and Eve stopped being thankful, when there was no more leaping into the arms of God's love, it says they became futile in their thoughts. Giving of thanks is not a footnote; giving of thanks is not a P.S. Futility means pointless, meaningless, going around in circles. When a person is not giving thanks, their thoughts become actions that result in absolute futility. I see a direct correlation between the need to consume material goods and the absolute futility many of my clients feel after their purchases. Buying becomes a sport and/or an addiction without any regard to being thankful for each possession. This direct lack of respect (unthankfulness) is a beginning of clutter build-up. Have you ever heard your clients mutter, unable to comprehend the process because of the sheer magnitude of the clutter? "…and their foolish hearts were darkened." The absence of thanksgiving is a heart of self-will or self-effort, everything that goes with the lie.

The giving of thanks joins us to divine wisdom and purpose. Giving thanks is the very oxygen of indwelling with God. Giving thanks is a valuable treasure.

"...to proclaim your love in the morning and your faithfulness at night..." Psalm 92:2 (NIV)

Let us give thanks every morning for the mercies of the night, and every night for the mercies of the day; going out, and coming in, let us bless God.

I have a client who called me for time management skills. As a Christian client, I asked her if she spent any time in prayer before the day began. This happened to be on her wish list. Her current days are filled with meaningless activities, but ones she feels obligated to do for her family's sake. I asked her to do an experiment before getting out of bed. I asked her to write down three things she was thankful for yesterday and three things she was thankful for today. As she took authority over her hours, her attitude reflected the naming of the day. It was no longer just another day. As the weeks progressed, her heart began to change, and new directions began to take shape in her life. Her hours were filled with purpose, meaning, and a renewed thankfulness.

May we all be intentional in our giving of thanks. May we be continually reminded that man's fall separated us from God's amazing love in many ways, most importantly our desire to give thanks. Jesus came to restore that broken heart and give us the supernatural desire to leap into the Father's arms again. This good news is too good to keep under a basket. Let this thanksgiving light so shine as you pass it onto another. I pray your days are filled with purpose, intent, and abundant thanksgiving.

The Eye of the Needle:
Bigger than you Think
Eileen Koff

"Again I tell you, it is easier for a camel to go through the eye of a needle than for someone who is rich to enter the kingdom of God." Matthew 19:24 (NIV)

Matthew 19:24 is one of the most iconic scriptures of the New Testament and one I've used often to illustrate the impossibility of finding peace and order unless you're unwilling to unburden yourself of encumbering worldly possessions.

Translation: You can't get organized if you aren't willing to throw stuff away. This is a difficult truth for many to accept, especially those who have acquired a lifetime of material goods. The more stuff someone has, the more unwilling they generally are to get rid of it, and the harder it is for them to achieve the peaceful life they seek.

We often think of Jesus speaking in parables like this to explain His teachings, so I've always taken for granted the impossibility of this image. A camel, literally slipping through the eye of a needle? I mean, come on. No chance at all, right?

However, scholars have theorized that the needle Jesus was referring to was actually the Needle Gate, a small opening in the wall surrounding Jerusalem. At night, when the main gates were locked, city-keepers would allow camels and their owners to come in via the Needle Gate, which, for security purposes, forced owners to first remove any saddles or packs from the camel before the animal could slip through.

As a professional organizer, I rejoice at this revelation. It still means that to enter the City of God, one has to first unshackle himself of the stuff he carries. But it's not as ludicrously impossible as it first appeared. What was once pure allegory is now much more accessible.

Organizing is a two-step process. First, one must recognize today's priorities and the needs that fit within that priority. Having the ability to let go of those things, be it objects, activities, or people that no longer fit into your lifestyle, is essential before any organization can take place.

Giving up your stuff is never easy. Not for me, not for anybody. Take time to focus on what is truly important in your life. By keeping God at the center of our lives and by coming to Him in prayer, He will direct our steps toward what is essential for our lives today and away from what is no longer serving our purposes. It truly is amazing how much clearer one can hear His still small voice in a room free of distractions and clutter. If road-weary travelers truly did thread the eye of the needle to get into the city, we can certainly clean out our sock drawer.

His Loving Touch
Tracy Axcell

"A man with leprosy came to him and begged him on his knees, 'If you are willing, you can make me clean.'" Mark 1:40 (NIV)

Leprosy is an awful disease. The Old Testament contains lengthy rules and laws regarding how to deal with disease and those who had contact with anyone diseased. The life of a leper was lonely, as they were isolated from everyone who wasn't infected. They were cast out to the outskirts of town, removed from worship in the temple, and no longer allowed human contact with anyone, including family!

The leper who approached Jesus in Mark 1:40 was such a man. Kneeling before Jesus, in utter humility, he pleaded, "If You are willing, You can make me clean." This leper knew the law and knew he was breaking the law in approaching a clean man—not just any clean man, but Jesus the Teacher and Healer! The leper could have been severely punished—but really, what did he have to lose?

Look at Jesus' love toward this leper: "Then Jesus, moved with compassion, stretched out His hand and touched him." Jesus touched him! He knowingly touched an unclean man—making Himself ceremonially unclean! With compassion, Jesus touched this man who'd not received a hug, a kiss, a gentle pat, or a touch for who knows how long—he was touched and made whole by Jesus. "As soon as He had spoken, immediately the leprosy left him, and he was cleansed."

Jesus told the cleansed leper to go quietly and first allow the Priests to see him. Jesus wanted him to do things the lawful way so he could be declared clean and welcomed back to the temple and society. Why didn't he obey? What would you do if you'd just received the ability to have human contact and socialize again? I'd do exactly what the leper did—run to my family, hug everyone, and announce to the world that I'd been healed!

Was it pride, over-exuberance, or just plain old disobedience that caused him to ignore Jesus' command? I don't know, but I do know this— disobedience on his part meant Jesus now had to live "outside, in lonely places." Jesus and the leper swapped places.

I can't help but think of our clients who feel isolated and even ridiculed by family and society; they feel like outcasts. They so desperately want to be "healed." And so, they reach out, in humility, and ask you and me to help them.

We are given an opportunity to love like Jesus, to reach out and hug them, encourage them, and show them the way to healing. And in a small way, we too exchange places with them. We take on their burden. We become "unclean" as we work with them in their spaces. And we are there as their life is transformed!

Are you willing to reach out and "touch" your client today so they can be healed and maybe even be touched by Jesus through you? What an amazing gift of mercy, love, and grace you and I are given by God!

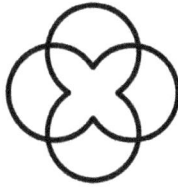

The Butterfly Effect
Eileen Koff

"So will it be with the resurrection of the dead. The body that is sown is perishable, it is raised imperishable; it is sown in dishonor, it is raised in glory; it is sown in weakness, it is raised in power; it is sown a natural body, it is raised a spiritual body." 1 Corinthians 15:42-44 (NIV)

"For the trumpet will sound, the dead will be raised imperishable, and we will be changed." 1 Corinthians 15:52b (NIV)

The butterfly has long been a Christian symbol of resurrection, for the caterpillar disappears into a cocoon and appears dead, but after many weeks, the butterfly emerges far more beautiful and powerful than before.

In my early Christian walk, my best conversations with Jesus were in a garden that I created to attract butterflies. This summer it attracted a large number of cabbage moths. I marveled at what seemed like a hundred white wings floating in the air. In my longing for a deeper understanding, I asked our Lord to teach me something I didn't know about His butterflies. What I found in my search (Wikipedia) was the "butterfly effect."

The phrase refers to the idea that the flapping of a butterfly's wings creates tiny changes in the atmosphere that may ultimately alter the path of a weather event as large as a tornado. The flapping wing represents a small change in the initial condition of the system, which causes a chain of events leading to large-scale alterations of events. Had the butterfly not flapped its wings, the trajectory of the system might have been vastly different.

Wow! We create butterfly effects too. Professional organizers create tiny changes in our clients' lives that ultimately alter the path of their tornado (or chaos). Our convergence with their lives may even prevent the occurrence of devastating circumstances. Small initial changes often do lead to greater transforming patterns in their lives. You have seen the effect when we clear a space—the mind becomes more focused, and then a healthier outlook follows. Better food preparation, family management, and less chaotic time schedules are some of the changes we witness. Conversely, if we had not entered our clients' lives, one can only imagine the chaos that would continue, not only within the space but also in the relationships in the home. We might also consider the ripple effect that occurs when a client tells a friend about his/her experience, and so on and so on. What a mighty God we serve!

Lord, it is my prayer that those reading this will meditate on how their butterfly effect has created an amazing ripple within their sphere of influence. As each Faithful Organizer goes forth to the calling that you have set before us, may we never underestimate the power of this calling. We may never see all the accomplishments that we initiated by our presence, but even the tiniest of movements can cause amazing transformations when guided by your Holy Spirit.

"Not by might nor by power, but by my Spirit say the Lord." Zechariah 4:6 (NIV)

It's Not You; It's Me

Angie Hyche

"For we do not have a high priest who is unable to empathize with our weaknesses, but we have one who has been tempted in every way, just as we are—yet he did not sin. Let us then approach God's throne of grace with confidence, so that we may receive mercy and find grace to help us in our time of need."
Hebrews 4:15-16 (NIV)

The nature of our work as professional organizers allows us to get to know our clients extremely well. In many sessions, we're working one-on-one with clients, sorting through belongings, and sometimes having very meaningful and private conversations. There's nothing like sorting through treasured keepsakes and underwear to forge a connection with someone! Our conversations can be intense, sometimes dealing with deep psychological issues. If the work occurs over a long period, our professional relationship may start to feel like a friendship.

Because of the close bond that develops when the working relationship ends, it can feel like personal rejection, especially if the ending lacks closure. Clients sometimes simply drift away, suddenly failing to answer our emails, phone calls, or texts without any explanation. We're left scratching our heads, wondering if we did or said something to offend them. We may think that if we had done a better job, they wouldn't have disappeared.

During Jesus' time on earth, He experienced every emotion that we do. Jesus faced rejection constantly, so He's quite familiar with the emotions it

103

generates. Jesus knew that even when people rejected Him, ultimately, they weren't rejecting Him, but the Father.

"The one who hears you hears me, and the one who rejects you rejects me, and the one who rejects me rejects him who sent me." Luke 10:16 (NIV)

Jesus knew that the rejection wasn't about Him. In a similar vein, when our clients end our working relationship, it's usually *not* about us.

There are a multitude of reasons our clients stop working with us, including but not limited to the following: lack of funds, conflict with others in the home about the services, a hectic schedule, a changing life situation, shifting priorities, or simply an unwillingness to make changes in their habits.

Whatever the reason, talking about it with peers who understand is invaluable! That's one of the best things about Faithful Organizers. We can truly understand each other's joys and struggles. God created us to be in community with other believers because He knew how much we needed that support.

While we gain tremendous support from each other, the best medicine of all is pouring our hearts out to God about both the small annoyances and the crushing heartaches. God loves us more than we can comprehend, and He really does care about even the most trivial concerns.

Reach out to each other and reach out to God. He's given you all the support you need for every situation you face.

All Things New
Eileen Koff

"The latter glory of this house will be greater than the former . . . and in this place I shall give peace . . . " Haggai 2:9 (ESV)

I recently read the book of Ezra. I encourage you to read the magnificent story of the rebuilding of the temple. In chapter 10:10-13, there is a strange occurrence that divides the generations. The young, seeing the temple finally completed, praised God with a LOUD voice, but the elders, recalling the glory of Solomon's temple, wept. Between the rejoicing and the weeping, the noise was deafening. But the Lord came and spoke these words to them:

"The latter glory of this house will be greater than the former...and in this place I shall give peace..." Haggai 2:9

In a similar way, the Lord comes into our lives and makes "All Things New." As professional organizers, we have the opportunity to demonstrate this same transformation in people's lives in practical ways. The Lord uses our natural gifts and talents of organizing to come into a space and create order where there was once chaos. Through our gifts, the Lord allows us to create possibilities of a new life, new hope, and fulfilled dreams.

Many times, our clients wonder if a new beginning is possible. "Where do I start?" they ask. The thought of a new beginning can also be frightful—because as humans, we dislike change, even good change. Our clients may become stuck, unable to proceed because they want the life they knew in the past, much like the elders who envisioned Solomon's temple, but they did not understand the glory that awaited them in the humble, yet spirit-filled presence of God in the new. The process of organizing may seem daunting to our clients, but with our leading, when peace, hope, and life re-enter their homes, businesses, and lives, they will praise God!

"Trust Me and lean not on your own understanding. In all your ways acknowledge Me, and I will direct your paths straight. When I delight in your ways, I will make your steps firm. I know the plans I have for you, plans to prosper you and not to harm you, plans for a future and a hope."

"My Word is a light in your path and a lamp for your feet. Whoever loses his life for My name's sake will find it. Allow me to make all things new in your life."

The Lord is pleased when we trust Him in all areas of our lives. He is also pleased when we encourage and support one another, which is what Faithful Organizers is all about—being faithful to Him and one another.

Every day we have opportunities to be the salt and light of hope and life to those around us. We are His instruments of peace. Many times, we ourselves also need this same peace and experience of new hope, new life, and new beginnings. Allow God to make all things new in your life, to use you as His servants to make all things new in the lives of the people we so graciously and passionately serve.

Now, may our Lord God bless you and keep you, may he make his face shine upon you and be gracious to you, and as he makes all things new, may you find peace.

The Power of a Comforter
Seana Turner

What is your favorite time of day? I used to have a little dog named Precious, and her favorite time of day was bedtime. She always got excited when it was time for me to lift her up and onto my bed. (Yes, I admit it; I let her sleep in my bed.) Every night she would jump and paw at the side of the bed, tail wagging furiously, full of anticipation. Once I had placed her on the bed, she loved to dance upon and ultimately burrow into my fluffy comforter. Finally, she would let out a sigh of contentment and go to sleep.

I must admit that I often feel the same way about getting into bed. Snuggling down under my comforter on a cool night makes me feel safe and warm. Under my comforter, as the cares of the day subside, I can let go, relax, and just be myself.

Recently I was reading John 14:26, where Jesus says:

"But the Advocate, the Holy Spirit, whom the Father will send in My name, will teach you everything, and will remind you all that I have said to you." (NRSV)

Wow—I love this verse! Jesus is telling the disciples that His leaving (which seems in the moment to be the worst possible thing that could happen) will instead be a tremendous blessing. Why? Because once Jesus has ascended, the Holy Spirit will arrive, pouring into the disciples all kinds of wonderfulness.

The Greek word for the Holy Spirit in this verse—*Paracletes*—can be translated as helper, advocate, or *comforter*. When I see the word "comforter,"

I immediately flash back to my dog, curled up in complete peace and joy. Like her, we can rest in the knowledge that God is in control, guiding us with perfect knowledge, strength, and energy. God knows exactly what the plan is and how to accomplish it. What a comfort!

In a way, God enables us to play a similar role with our clients. When we bring our gifts and talents to our clients, we automatically become "little comforters." Clients can exhale and relax because we will do the hard part. For example, we offer:

Vision, because we can see the end result of the project.

Experience, so we aren't thrown off by tough decisions or challenging circumstances.

Energy, because we are excited about what we know can be accomplished.

Focus, since we are committed to the task at hand.

As we bring our skills to bear, our clients can trust us, and in turn they can release the worry and anxiety of having to figure it all out on their own. We may not be perfect like the Lord, but we do "come alongside to help."

After promising the coming of the Holy Spirit, Jesus goes on in verse 27 to say:

"Peace I leave with you; my peace I give to you. I do not give to you as the world gives. Do not let not your hearts be troubled, and do not let them be afraid." (NRSV)

The result of having the Comforter in our lives is peace. Not the peace that the world offers through material gain, beauty, status, or power—all of which are fleeting at best. Instead, the Comforter provides the inner contentment that comes from knowing we are loved and accepted just as we are, even as we are *"instructed and counseled in the way we should go."* (Psalm 32:8)

As we work with our clients, many of whose hearts are troubled and afraid, may we emulate the great Comforter and serve as conduits of peace. May we blanket our clients with acceptance, even as we direct and help them. May our patience and love make our presence their "favorite time of day," and in so doing, may we give glory to the One who chose to pour out help and comfort upon all who seek Him.

Thank God for the Trailblazers
Angie Hyche

"To this you were called, because Christ suffered for you, leaving you an example, that you should follow in his steps." I Peter 2:21 NIV

Hiking is one of my favorite activities. I particularly love hiking on a wooded, creek-side trail. The sound of the gently running water, the shade, and the beauty of the forest are very soothing.

If you spend much time hiking, you learn to look for trail markers. Trail markers can be made from a pile of rocks, a wooden post, an etching, or a nailed sign. However, the most common marker is a blaze, a simple rectangular paint swipe on a tree trunk. By simply going from one blaze to the next, you can be sure you're on the right path.

It's usually easy to stay on a trail by following the blazes. But occasionally they are difficult to follow. Perhaps the paint has faded, some trees have fallen or been burned, or the blazes aren't spaced closely enough. As long as you have enough food and water, a good GPS or map, and enough daylight, you'll be okay. If not, you could be in danger.

When hiking a well-marked trail, I'm grateful for those who have gone before me, clearing the trail and painting the blazes so that I can safely navigate. I feel secure as I hike because of the work others have done to make sure the route is obvious.

Wouldn't it be wonderful if we had blazes to follow in our everyday lives? We'd be assured that we're on the correct path and that we'd reach our destination safely. In a way, we do! Jesus came to earth to blaze the trail for us, showing us how to live. He's our trailblazer.

"To this you were called, because Christ suffered for you, leaving you an example, that you should follow in his steps." I Peter 2:21 (NIV)

If we follow Jesus' steps deliberately, looking to His example and emulating His lifestyle, we can rest assured that we are following the path God has laid out for us. But what does that mean practically?

Jesus didn't have exactly the same kind of life as us. He didn't own a small business, help clients declutter and organize, or give a presentation on a paper organizing system.

But Jesus did lead a group of believers. He did meet people who needed His help to make changes in their lives. And He had numerous opportunities to speak to crowds.

Following Jesus' steps requires us to study His interactions in the context of His life on Earth and to consider how we can put those same principles into practice.

When we follow Jesus' steps, we strive to be as much like Him as possible. Jesus was (and is) God in the flesh, a physical representation of the character of our Father.

"The Son radiates God's own glory and expresses the very character of God, and he sustains everything by the mighty power of his command." Hebrews 1:3 (NLT)

I'm so grateful that God has given us such an amazing trailblazer. I want to follow so closely that I put my feet directly in the path He blazed. I want to remind my clients of Jesus. I want to follow His example of leading people to God and of glorifying God in all that I do.

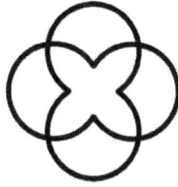

Vision for Your Business
Sangita Evans and Angie Hyche

"Whatever you do, work at it with all your heart, as working for the Lord, not for human masters, since you know that you will receive an inheritance from the Lord as a reward. It is the Lord Christ you are serving." Colossians 3:23-24 (NIV)

The emotional burden of a business owner can be a heavy one. Even if you have plenty of support, it can still feel overwhelming to know that for the most part, the buck stops with you. Without the predictability of a regular schedule, we may feel as if we are constantly "on the job." And when we're faced with a lengthy list of tasks with a small amount of available time, it can be discouraging.

How can we accomplish our goals for our businesses while navigating the sense of overwhelm that threatens to paralyze us? How do we decide which dreams to pursue relentlessly, and which ones are meant for another time, if any? How can we stay in tune with God's Spirit so that we know the difference between a golden God-given opportunity and a plan whose time hasn't yet come?

I don't pretend to know the answers. But I have learned a few things over the past six years as a business owner, and I pray that these thoughts help others. I've got three points that all start with the letter "L" to make them easier to remember.

Lay Down Your Burden

If you feel a constant heavy weight on your back, that burden isn't from God. Perhaps you've loaded too much weight on yourself. God may be directing you to let some of it go.

"Take my yoke upon you and learn from me, for I am gentle and humble in heart, and you will find rest for your souls. For my yoke is easy and my burden is light."

Matthew 11:29-30 (NIV)

We can't do everything! When we try to do too much, we aren't nearly as effective as we could be. We're scattered and exhausted. That's no way to live, and it's not God's plan to live that way. This is a truth that I have to constantly revisit. I have a terrible tendency to take on too much. It's not healthy for me, and it's not healthy for you either.

Is it time to let go of something good so that you can accomplish something great? Are you praying for wisdom and discernment?

Learn God's Special Plan for You

Ask God to show you the works He has prepared in advance that only you can do. And try to focus on only those works.

"For we are God's handiwork, created in Christ Jesus to do good works, which God prepared in advance for us to do." Ephesians 2:10 (NIV)

This Scripture is a favorite. I find it amazing that God has already lined up tasks that only we are perfectly equipped to do. I want to be sure to find those and do them! I'll be smack dab in the center of His will for my life, and I'm practically guaranteed to succeed because I'm set up to win by the Creator of the Universe Himself!

Listen for His Voice

Listen for God's voice. He speaks in so many different ways! It could be any of the following (or even more!): Scripture, an answer to prayer, an unanswered prayer, someone else's words, a circumstance, a gut feeling, a thought, something you see, a memory, a dream. There is no limit to the ways God's Spirit can try to get our attention.

When we pray for discernment and God's leading, we've got to be sure we're paying attention to His answer! If we're overloaded, we might miss it. If we're easily distracted with a cluttered mind, it may fly under our radar. The answer might take a while, and it might not take the form you expect. Be ready!

I'm thankful that God is persistent! Many times, when God has given me a vision, I've been prompted over and over in different ways. It's an idea that won't seem to go away. That was the case with starting my business and with writing my book, *Unholy Mess: What the Bible Says about Clutter*. In fact, a repeated message is one of the ways I know an idea is coming from God.

Are you ready to lay down your burden, to learn God's individual plan for you, and to listen for His voice? His yoke is easy. He's got the deck stacked in your favor. And He longs to give you the purpose and peace you need. You just have to ask.

March on Abigails!

Sangita Evans

"Charm is deceptive, and beauty is fleeting; but a woman who fears the Lord is to be praised. Honor her for all that her hands have done, and let her works bring her praise at the city gate." Proverbs 31:30-31 (NIV)

The Bible is full of remarkable, godly women that displayed extraordinary strength and power. Take, for instance, this intelligent and beautiful woman named Abigail.

In 1 Samuel 25, Abigail was unfortunately married to Nabal, who was surly and mean in his dealings. Although he was blessed with property and wealth, he was not generous or kind. There was a time when David's men were kind to Nabal's servants as they herded their sheep into the desert. David's men even sheltered them and watched over their property. But when David asked for some provision for his men and himself, Nabal did not reciprocate that same kindness. Instead, Nabal insulted them and turned them away. This enraged David, and he swore to kill Nabal and all the men in his family, obliterating his name altogether! Luckily, in stepped Abigail, a woman of initiative, courage, and faith.

Abigail was dealt a challenging life situation, but she showed the strength of character that overcame difficult circumstances instead of being overcome by them. She could've been miserable, discouraged, or depressed about being married to such a wicked man. But instead, she took on the attitude to be solution-oriented, not procrastinate, and was a quick thinker. She was wise, courageous, and also humble in resolving this difficult situation with King David.

- She was not intimidated by the huge army she would face. **(She didn't get overwhelmed.)**
- She didn't even stop to think if she could make a difference in such an impossible situation. **(She didn't feel insignificant or have self-doubt.)**
- She didn't stop to think how David or Nabal would respond. **(She wasn't a people pleaser.)**
- Instead, by faith, she persevered with a plan of action. **(She was a planner!)**
- Perhaps the most important aspect of overcoming her difficult situation was her dependence on God's truths. **(God was her source of strength; she listened to what He instructed her to do.)**
- She brought out the good in David and reminded him to be faithful to God's truths. **(Her life impacted others.)**
- Her humble response, taking the blame for her husband's behavior, and risking her life was the result of allowing herself to be taught by the heart of God. **(She didn't get defensive or prideful.)**

Let's change our perspectives and apply this to our clients, who are also in a challenging situation. They too may not have the support of their family and friends as they are dealing with the mountain of clutter and chaos in their lives. Perhaps they only see what they are up against and feel hopeless.

I believe God is calling us professional organizers to step in on their behalf and be their "Abigail." Because we hold to God's truths, we know we can overcome anything through Him who strengthens us. We train ourselves to be taught by the heart of God. We then have the eyes to see and ears to hear His direction—not only for our lives, but for our clients as well. God gives us the wisdom to handle each situation and see the victory that our clients cannot see. Like Abigail, we can be quick and creative problem solvers. We can see past the mountains of clutter and chaos and bring our clients peace.

What does today's modern-day woman look like? What will they say about them 50 years from now? Well, today's modern-day **Christian** woman is full of strength and power—just like Abigail! She is courageous, relies on God, and holds onto His truths. She does not procrastinate. She makes the best of her situation. She brings out the best in others. She is willing to humble herself and risk her life to help someone more undeserving. She is—YOU!

When we are faced with challenging situations or are stuck in a circumstance that may not change, do we respond righteously and quickly?

Ambassadors of Love

Angie Hyche

We all yearn desperately to be loved. Some of us are blessed to have people in our lives to partially satisfy this longing. But ultimately, every single one of us will be disappointed by a loved one at one time or another, many of us repeatedly. As imperfect humans, we are simply incapable of loving perfectly.

Oh, but we are most certainly loved perfectly by our Heavenly Father. His love is unconditional, all-consuming, beyond our wildest imagination. He knows everything about us, even the parts we want to hide because we're ashamed. He knows all the things we've used to try to fill that void inside our hearts. He knows every word we've spoken in anger, every missed opportunity, every time we've run away from Him. And He still loves us.

The following two Scriptures paint a beautiful picture of God's incomparable love:

"And I pray that you, being rooted and established in love, may have power, together with all the Lord's holy people, to grasp how wide and long and high and deep is the love of Christ, and to know this love that surpasses knowledge—that you may be filled to the measure of all the fullness of God." Eph. 3:17-19 (NIV)

"The Lord is compassionate and merciful,
slow to get angry and filled with unfailing love.
He will not constantly accuse us,
nor remain angry forever.

He does not punish us for all our sins;
    He does not deal harshly with us, as we deserve.
For his unfailing love toward those who fear him
    is as great as the height of the heavens above the earth.
He has removed our sins as far from us
    as the east is from the west.
The Lord is like a father to his children,
    tender and compassionate to those who fear him."

Ps. 103:8-13 (NLT)

When Jesus came to the Earth, He put love into action. He was the embodiment of God's love in human flesh. As John 1:14 recounts, *"The Word became flesh and made his dwelling among us."* (NIV) He showed us how to love while He was here on earth. When He returned to the Father, He charged us with the responsibility of being God's representatives, to love each other just as God loves us.

What an intimidating task we've been given! I don't know about you, but many days, I just don't feel capable. I think perhaps God should just choose someone else for the job. But here's the catch—there are people who need God's love that only you and I can reach. God's plan is for Christians to spread His love in their specific spheres of influence, to act as the hands and feet of Jesus. We're not just part of God's plan. We ARE the plan.

As a Christian professional organizer, we have the awesome responsibility and the privilege of demonstrating God's love to our clients. They've been entrusted to us for a time, and we are called to love them just like God loves us, just like Jesus modeled for us.

I've noticed that many of my clients seem beaten down by the world. They are ashamed of their clutter and disorganization, and they feel like a failure. Just reaching out to us for help is a huge step. And now, we get to love on them. We get to show them they are worthy of our time and our attention, that they deserve to live in a peaceful home. We get to show them a better way to live. While they're in our care, we can shower them with God's love and watch them flourish.

Oh, sisters, don't think for a minute that your job is unimportant. We have the most extraordinary mission of all. We are representatives of the King of Kings.

"And whatever you do or say, do it as a representative of the Lord Jesus, giving thanks through him to God the Father." Colossians 3:17 (NLT)

Founders'
Witness
Testimonials

Jean Furuya

My first recollection of being connected to God was when I was five years old and attending Catholic school. Although I'm sure my mother took me to church on Sundays, I only remember being in church when I went to confession at school over the next three years. I'm not sure, but I believe I made up things to confess! When we switched to a Protestant church, I was relieved to learn I could talk to God directly. Of course, by that time I didn't have to make up anything; I had plenty to confess! Some people have dramatic testimonials of mountaintop experiences during which they accepted Christ and immediately turned their lives around 180 degrees. My story is not so dramatic, but it is no less significant that I chose to follow my Lord and Savior.

While my life has not been completely smooth sailing, I am thankful that there have been no devastating storms. I have felt God's presence with me for as long as I can remember. Any difficulties I have had were caused by my being strong-willed, egocentric, and impatient. So much of my life has been more about my wanting to do things *my* way rather than *God's* way! I have always been grateful and thankful as the Lord has been my anchor—keeping me from straying too far from Him.

Like so many people, I claim Romans 8:28: *"And we know that in all things God works for the good of those who love Him, who have been called according to His purpose."* Gradually over the years I've mellowed, becoming more kind, caring, patient, better at seeking God's will, etc. Thankfully, God continues to bless me and make good however I mess up.

I didn't wait on the Lord for my spouse, and I had a rude awakening after I got married. You've heard the expressions "love is blind" or "hindsight is 20/20" or "all you need is love," etc.? Well, I quickly came to realize that my husband was an 18th century Samurai man, and I was a 20th century independent woman. Unfortunately for him, I wasn't the typical submissive Japanese wife. We were like oil and vinegar. The two ingredients naturally repel each other, but when agitated and infused by blending or shaking, they come together to create a beautiful bouquet that smells and tastes divine! Because of our commitment to each other, respect for our differences, and by the grace of God, despite my self-reliance, we both feel thankful and blessed for our 60 years of marriage!

In 1991, I started my organizing business. When I had decided to leave the small company I worked for after 12 years, a co-worker mentioned that since I organized everything in the company, I should see about becoming an organizer. Her boyfriend belonged to a networking group in which another organizer was a member. I called the organizer and became excited about the prospect of having my own business! Starting the business was easy; getting clients was another story! After a few months, I began thinking maybe I wasn't meant to be in the organizing business. I asked God that if He wanted me to stay in the business, to please provide me with clients—which He did!

In the same year, I also joined the National Association of Productivity and Organizing Professionals (NAPO). Several years later, it was such a blessing getting together with other Christian organizers at the Orlando NAPO conference. Every year thereafter, someone attending the conference would post a time for devotion and/or prayer. Meetings were held in someone's room, auditorium, hallway, or wherever we could find a private space. Even though it was only once a year, I looked forward to being a part of that group. After a while I asked around about starting a formal group. But nothing came about until 2006, several months before the NAPO conference to be held in Boston. God had brought all the key players together. And with the help of the NAPO management company (who were Christians), we were given the use of one of the meeting rooms to hold our devotional and prayer times before the conference started each day. We even had speakers! In 2009, Faithful Organizers officially became an association. And in September 2012, we held our own conference in Chicago the day before the Institute for Challenging Disorganization (ICD) conference started. John 15:4-5 says Jesus is the vine and we are the branches, and if we remain in Him, we will bear much fruit. I continue to pray that as His ambassadors and the branches connected to Him, Faithful Organizers will bear much fruit for His kingdom.

When I first started my business, I said I did not want to work with chronically disorganized clients. Being left-brained, I just wanted to "fix/organize" my clients' various situations. In time I realized it was those who were challenged by chronic disorganization who needed the most help. Once I changed my attitude and started helping them, I found it very rewarding (although sometimes very tough!), and I became more compassionate, caring, and patient.

When I turned 65, I thought about retiring. As I waited for an answer from God, an organizer contacted me saying that she was changing careers and asked if I would be interested in working with the cognitive therapist with whom she had been working. I became intrigued, especially when I found out she was a Christian therapist. I felt this was an answer to prayer.

As I've entered the sunset years, God continues to use me and my organizing skills to be a blessing to whomever He puts in my path. I'm still not completely retired from working with clients, but I continue to wait on the Lord and His direction for the rest of my life.

Barbara Hemphill

I grew up on a farm in Nebraska. We lived in three rooms on the 2nd floor of a tenant farmhouse. My father's parents lived on the first floor. My brother and I slept in the living room on a couch that we pulled out into two separate beds. The bathroom was on the first floor.

We went to our small country church every Sunday morning, every Sunday evening, and every Wednesday evening. Only a severe illness would keep us away! Daddy came in from milking the cows to join us for breakfast, after which we always read a devotion from The Upper Room. I was often bored—even annoyed—at the ritual. My grandfather often said, "God told me...." His statement unsettled me because no matter how many times I went to the altar during revival meetings to ask God to speak to me, I never heard Him. Once I recall Grandad saying, "If you don't hear from God, it's because you have skeletons in your closet." I have joked that perhaps I started my business as an organizing consultant cleaning out closets in a desperate attempt to hear God.

In college, I met a young man who was planning to be in the ministry. He was the fourth in a family of seven children where God seemed to be very active. We married, traveled around the world serving God, adopted three orphan children, and returned to the U.S. Four years later, he asked for a divorce. I was devastated. No one in my family was divorced, and I felt if this man of God divorced me, I must have done something terrible to offend God. I continued to go to church, out of habit—rather than belief—and began exploring New Age teachings.

At that time, my best friend was Jewish and, much to my amazement, she accepted Jesus as her Savior. A few years later, the two of us went to a beach house to spend some time writing. On the way, we stopped at a small Christian bookstore in the country. My friend asked the owner where she went to church. The owner invited us to attend, and we agreed. When we walked into the church, we were shocked to see a variety of nationalities, but most surprising of all was sitting down behind a man wearing a yarmulke! During the service, the pastor invited people who wanted to dedicate their life to Christ to come forward. I did.

My life as a Christian continued to be rocky. At the age of 11, I had tried to commit suicide as a result of bullying in the small country school I attended. In my 40s, remarried but still struggling with depression, I admitted myself to New Life Center. I felt relieved because I was finally in an environment where I didn't have to prove anything to anyone or cover up my real feelings.

One experience in that environment changed my life forever. The art therapist asked me to draw a picture or do a collage, answering three questions: 1) How do I see myself? 2) How do others see me? 3) How does God see me? During the process of illustrating my answers, I saw the famous painting of Jesus knocking on the door. At that moment, I realized that God had offered His Son to me, but I had refused because I felt unworthy.

Ironically, from the beginning, my organizing business has been based on four words: "Clutter is postponed decisions." Ironically, I had to decide that God loved me—regardless of how I felt. That decision took me down a beautiful new path of discovering the peace and joy that comes from knowing God's eternal love—and sharing it with others!

On my tombstone will be the words, "She gave others hope." As a Christian, our eternal hope is Jesus Christ. As an entrepreneur and founder of Productive Environment Institute, my passion is offering others H.O.P.E. (Helping Others Pursue Entrepreneurship). When I first began my business, I prayed that my clients would feel the love of Jesus from me, whether I ever mentioned His name. For decades, I didn't because I was afraid of offending someone. When I celebrated my 70th birthday, I decided it was time to change my strategy. Today, I look for every opportunity to share how accepting God's gift of Jesus changed my life forever.

Eileen Koff

As a young Jewish girl, I would sit in Synagogue every Saturday for Hebrew school. During the service, I would gaze at the 30-foot Torah curtain and think, "They're not telling me everything!" I knew there must be more to Judaism than what my teachers were teaching. This led me to study Kabbalah, which is Jewish mysticism, and other occult studies such as astrology, tarot readings, UFOlogy, paranormal activity, etc.

After graduating from college, I married, and within a few years, moved with my husband and sons to Bethesda, Maryland. Shortly after moving in, a neighbor knocked at our front door. Her boy was the same age as Evan and thought they should have a play date. She began telling me that she had a "weird" experience that maybe she shouldn't share, but she had no one else to tell it to.

Loving the "weird" world of the paranormal, I was intrigued. She told me about the experience of a man showing up in her home, apparently out of nowhere. She asked his name. He said "Jesus" and then was gone. She asked me how to find out more about Jesus. I told her I was Jewish, and she said she was an atheist. I said the only way to learn about Jesus is the Bible, but not the Bible I knew. She said, "Let's meet at my house every Friday and read that Bible." Our sessions together spring-boarded our learning about Jesus, and within a few months, we both came to accept Jesus as Lord!

Since my baptism in July 1990, God has taken me on many paths. Because of my knowledge of the occult, I was very aware of the supernatural realm and the many encounters I was experiencing as a new believer. Within a year, I became acquainted with the Sentinel Group in Seattle and learned their "spiritual mapping" technique. Because spiritual mapping focuses on community transformations, it was natural that many asked me into homes for spiritual cleansing. It was through this path that God led me into the professional organizing industry because I began to notice a common factor, that the spiritual and the natural are very closely tied. How we live our daily lives, how we spend our time, our resources and even our relationships have a profound effect on our spiritual growth.

In Matthew 25:14-30, The Parable of the Talents, Jesus tells us that our gifts are given to us in order to affect the Kingdom. How well we multiply His gifts will impact us not only while we live here on earth, but into eternity. Our responsibilities given in eternity are a reflection of our talents!

What does this have to do with organizing? EVERYTHING!

The following are just two examples of the many that are revealed in my book, *Get Organized God's Way*.

Our relationships take front and center in all that we are and all that we do.

Luke 10:27 tells us, *"Love the Lord your God with all your heart and with all your soul and with all your strength and with all your mind"* and, *"Love your neighbor as yourself."*

Simply stated, a disorganized lifestyle suffocates relationships. Clutter has a way of isolating us from building and maintaining meaningful relationships. Instead of constructing a safe space, our clutter actually builds walls of isolation. We can miss the blessings of fellowship because of the shame and embarrassment a cluttered house evokes.

"He who is of God hears God's words." John 8:47

Hearing from God is paramount to your progress as a Christian, but clutter can shout over every attempt to hear God's still small voice. It's difficult to quiet the mind and hear from God under ordinary circumstances, but it's next to impossible to hear Him when stuff is competing for your attention. Many of my clients have expressed that when there is too much clutter in their space, they find it hard to hear or concentrate.

The world's daily distractions and material mindset impede our ability to develop the gifts that God has given us. I have found in every instance when organizing a home, mindset chains are broken, and peace is returned where chaos once reigned. The clarity of peace and purpose is enhanced.

Every path that God has led me on, from a seeking Jewish girl to today, has allowed me to grow the talents and responsibilities that God has imparted to me. My purpose as an organizer gave me the knowledge to write the Bible study *Get Organized God's Way* so that Christians worldwide can combat the world's lies, distortions, and distractions.

Sandy Wright

When I was a little girl, there were times I was frightened and felt alone. My dad was an alcoholic and my parents argued frequently. Being an only child, I didn't have anyone I could talk with about the troubles in my life. There were nights when I cried myself to sleep because of the sadness I felt. My "granny" took me to church with her, and that's probably where I learned about Jesus. He became my best friend and I would talk with Him often. I didn't feel alone when I was talking with Him. While I did not receive an audible response, I did receive peace and comfort.

At age 11, I accepted Christ as my Savior and my dad did, too. He was 42. We got baptized together. I received my own Bible and thought that was all I needed. I attended Sunday school and Church regularly, hearing the Bible lessons about all the people in the Bible. What I didn't understand was what I became when I accepted Jesus. I was a new creature and that meant I would begin thinking, behaving, and talking differently as a testimony to belonging to Him. That was the problem… I had accepted Jesus with my head, but not my heart.

Now at 11 I was not a bad or misbehaving child—according to the world's standards. In fact, I tried to be perfect. I did what was expected of me because I didn't want my mother or Dad being mad or disappointed. I thought that my behavior could help the tension in the house. I didn't understand about alcoholism and, like most children of alcoholics, I thought I could make things better if I did what I was supposed to do.

It wasn't hard doing what was expected of me because I loved school! I joined and did everything I could because it would get me out of the house and away from the fights and fear. On the outside, I was managing pretty well, but not on the inside. I was not progressing on my journey to be Christ-like. I would have told you that I was a Christian, but I truly didn't understand what that meant.

One of my coping skills was keeping my room orderly. If I couldn't control the circumstances in my life, I could control my space. My mom was organized and taught me skills at a young age. Planning my studying and projects came naturally to me.

In my 20s and early 30s, I turned away from Christ. I was hurt and disappointed after a divorce and didn't want to think about God. I had stopped going to church when I was in college and didn't attend until after I married again in 1979. I was convicted of what being a true Christian means one Sunday when the pastor was teaching from Luke 4:41, "Moreover, demons came out of many people, shouting, "You are the Son of God!" But he rebuked them and would not allow them to speak, because they knew he was the Messiah." The demons know who Christ is; they even fear Him; but they do not bow down (accept) Him as their Lord. Knowing who He is didn't make them a Christian.

My world was perfect...or so I thought. I had a wonderful husband, son, home, job, and friends. I was back in God's Word, worshiping at church, and making wonderful, godly friends. I had deep desires that only God knew. Although I loved my job, it meant long hours, and I wasn't home when our son got out of school. My first desire was that I could be home when he got out of school. The second desire was to participate in Bible study. At that time (early 80s) Bible studies were offered only during the day.

I was moving toward God and regaining my love for Jesus. Psalm 37:4, says, *"Take delight in the Lord, and he will give you the desires of your heart."* Those two desires that I had were pleasing to the Lord, and He answered my prayers...not quite the way that I thought! He was teaching me lessons that I needed to learn about my pride, lack of humility, and not trusting Him. The first lesson came when we lost our daughter, Sarah... But God wasn't through with me yet. He got me fired from my job. By that time, I was devastated!! On that day a dear friend called me and shared Romans 8:28, *"And we know that in all things God works for the good of those who love him, who have been called according to his purpose."* I could not immediately see it, but God was answering my "heart's desires" while at the same time drawing me closer and making me more Christ-like. He was using the job loss "for the good" to position me for my work as an organizer. I wasn't a Christian yet, though!

I had started Precept Bible Study and was soaking up the Word. I was asked to become a leader. To do so, I had to complete an application. In that document, I was asked to give my testimony and date when I became a Christian. I was trying to write down when I was 11, but literally, my hand could not touch the paper. As I reflected on what my life had been like from age 11 to then, I did not have a peace that I was truly saved. At that moment, I repented and surrendered to Jesus, making Him Lord of my life. The key word is "surrender" …letting Him lead my life. Not long after that, God blessed us with our daughter, Catherine! He knew I had one more heart's desire, and He granted it.

At that time a dear friend was going through an unwanted divorce and was depressed. Her emotional state was visible through the condition of her home. I called and said I was coming over to work on something… she was to pick it… a drawer, a closet... it didn't matter! After clearing out and reorganizing a closet, we both stood back. She announced how good that felt. Looking at her, I agreed, but for a different reason. I saw the peace on her face and the joy of having her closet usable again. From word of mouth, I started getting calls to help others and my organizing career was launched. God gifted me with innate abilities to be an organizer and opened the door through all my work experiences to have the skills to do the tasks. For me, my work is not a job, but a ministry because it gives me the opportunity to help people break free of the bondage of stuff and to understand that organization was designed by the Creator Himself.

About
the
Authors

Allison Mitchell resides with her husband in the Charlottesville, Virginia area. She has 2 grown sons and 2 doggies. She owns Allison Mitchell Organizing yet works full time as a Wound, Ostomy, and Continence Certified RN. She has walked with a variety of clients through organizing their home, businesses, paper, and estates. She believes chronic disorganization is a spiritual battle as well as an emotional and physical struggle.

Angie Hyche is a Certified Professional Organizer (CPO®), author, and speaker. She is passionate about helping readers unclutter their lives so they can focus on what matters most.

Her first book, *Unholy Mess: What the Bible Says about Clutter*, was published on Amazon in December 2020. Her second book, *Uncluttered: Shaping Your Home and Heart for What Matters Most*, co-authored with Liana George, will be published in June 2024 by Scrivenings Press.

In her free time, Angie enjoys exploring national parks with her husband, Eric, visiting their adult daughters Emma and Lydia, reading, and performing in community theatre. You can connect with Angie through email: angie@shipshape.solutions.

Ann Cueva, the owner of Custom Organizing, Inc., has been helping clients organize their homes and offices for the past 30 years. Ann is a Certified Productive Environment Specialist™ at the Productive Environment Institute. Ann is the author of the book, *Grief Without Chaos: Organization for Emergencies and Death*, a workbook for life's unexpected emergencies. A respected expert in paper, information, and time management, she engages in public speaking and conducts "customized" workshops tailored for your organization/company. She lives in Florida with her husband, John, and her family includes four children and one grandson. You can connect with Ann through her website: timeisthekey. com.

Barb Eimer is a freelance writer who owned an organizing business in Nashville for seven years before taking off to see the country in an RV.

She has six kids, eight grandkids, and currently lives in Indiana. You can reach her at barb@barbeimer.com. Her books are available on Amazon:

- *All My Favorite Colors are Red*—a humorous book on parenting
- *All My Favorite Heroes are Dead*—a Bible study on 10 Old Testament characters and what we can learn from their lives
- *Well Loved: Just As I Am*—a devotional for women

Barbara Hemphill, founder of Productive Environment Institute (PEI), launched her career in 1978 with a $7 ad in a New York newspaper, followed by her bestselling book *Taming the Paper Tiger*. Her world-class expertise is now delivered virtually by certified PEI Productive Environment specialists. Other books include *Less Clutter More Life* and the 20th Anniversary edition of *Love It or Lose It*. Barbara's current passion is offering Vision Accelerator coaching, empowering women to leave a legacy that matters! Her license plate reads HOPEFOOL: "I am a fool for Jesus, and H.O.P.E stands for Help Others Pursue Entrepreneurship." Connect with Barbara on her website: BarbaraHemphill.com.

Beta Shad is a full time kindergarten teacher and part-time professional organizer. She is a wellness advocate and her business, Living Tidy, focuses on the holistic benefits of clearing clutter and organizing. Her passion is educating people on how to keep their lives in order and enjoy well-being in all areas of their lives. You can connect with Beta through her website: livingtidy.com.

Beverly Clower is retired after an extensive career as a professional organizer specializing in office organization and paper management, based in the Los Angeles area. A lifelong Christian, she led a Bible study in her church for six years which was part of her inspiration to write a book about Jesus. *Jesus in the Dance of Life: Christ's Time on Earth* was published in January 2020. The publisher's promotional video can be seen at Youtube.com by searching there for her name. The book can be purchased with free shipping by request by emailing Beverly at Bevclower@gmail.com.

Donna Roland is a Christian women's speaker and stylist with a background in professional organizing. Donna is passionate about helping women embrace their beauty and self-confidence. She allows God to use her "life-learning" experiences to inspire women to find hope and joy through His strength and grace. With her Southern charm and humor, these experiences allow Donna the ability to empathize with women as she speaks from her heart and connects from the stage or working one-on-one to help them identify their own personal style. Donna resides in the Smoky Mountains of Tennessee with her husband, Jeff. Donna travels the United States speaking, styling, and consulting all year long! She can take you from a *cluttered, stressful wardrobe* to a *confident, stylish woman*!

Eileen Koff: I became a professional organizer with NAPO, (2007 received my CPO®) and shortly afterwards, founded Faithful Organizers with four sisters. As Faithful Organizers devotion and education director from 2007-2015, it was a blessing and honor to dive deeply into scripture and write a monthly devotion on what God says regarding an organized lifestyle. I believe there are many mental and emotional issues tied to clutter. However, at the root of clutter, there is a spiritual battle taking place, and very few organizers even go there or understand that when dealing with our clients. I pray as you read through these devotions, God will open the eyes of your understanding, and help you to shed His light into their dark places.

Kimberly Bignon is a native Kentuckian living in Orlando, Florida. In the year 2000, she took a leap of faith to start her own business, called Organize U. Kimberly's love for organizing and for people has taken her to many states over the years. Helping families and businesses win back time for the things that truly matter is her heart's desire. She has been a member of Faithful Organizers since 2012 and claims that her true identity is a "Disciple of Christ disguised as a Professional Organizer." When not organizing, Kimberly enjoys time with family and friends and watching her UK Wildcats. You can connect with her at organizeuco.com.

Lisa Dodson is a professional organizer and the owner of New Season Organizing. She has a passion for helping people, especially newly widowed or divorced women, with the decluttering process. She views her business as a ministry to share the love of Jesus, provide compassionate support and a listening ear. She lives in Fullerton, CA with her husband and German shepherd. When she is not working, she enjoys gardening, relaxing in the sun, and jigsaw puzzles. She is the current Executive Director of Faithful Organizers and has been an active board member for a number of years.

Michelle Kuiken, Organizer, Productivity Coach, and Farm Wife. Through her business, The Proper Place, she helps women break free from the overwhelm caused by busy schedules, cluttered lives, and trying to do it all. She creates simple solutions for the productivity and organizational challenges women face in trying to balance household, career, and life. Michelle has a holistic approach because she knows life doesn't fit into perfect, pretty containers. Understanding that everyone is different, she assesses a woman's situation and strengths in order to maximize efficiencies and minimize the overwhelm to make all parts of life flow smoother. Connect with her: properplace.life.

Sangita Evans owns Clear and Hear, a professional organizing company established in 2016. Sangita helps her clients clear the clutter and noise so they can hear the visions of their heart. She is a professional member of NAPO, the membership director of Faithful Organizers, and a member of the Professional Organizers of Long Island. Before starting her organizing career, Sangita was a medical billing director for an extensive pediatric practice. In addition to bringing order and clarity to her clients, she enjoys spending her spare time with her husband and two sons and leading women's Bible study groups.

Seana Turner has been a professional organizer since 2010. Her company The Seana Method provides freedom to clients by bringing order to time, space, and belongings. Seana assists clients in decluttering, establishing organized systems, improving productivity, managing their calendar, downsizing, and more.

Seana is a member of the National Association for Productivity and Organizing Professionals (NAPO), FOCUS Organizers of Fairfield County, and Faithful Organizers.

Seana offers in-person services throughout Fairfield County, Connecticut, and virtual services nationwide. For more information, visit TheSeanaMethod.com, and follow The Seana Method on Facebook, Instagram, Twitter, Pinterest, and YouTube.

Tracy Axcell has authored five devotionals and multiple in-depth Bible studies. Since retiring from organizing, she has had more time for her true passion: writing and teaching women's Bible studies and devotionals. Through her ministry, Forever His Bride, Tracy travels and speaks for women's groups around the country. She lives in Hot Springs Village, Arkansas with her husband of 42 years, Dennis. They have two children: James, who is in the Air Force, and Alicia, who, with her husband Tyler, has Tracy's first grandbaby, Benjamin.

www.ingramcontent.com/pod-product-compliance
Lightning Source LLC
Chambersburg PA
CBHW070931210326
41520CB00021B/6894